Contemporary English Literature

Edited by

R.P. Pradhan

ATLANTIC
PUBLISHERS & DISTRIBUTORS (P) LTD

Published by

ATLANTIC

PUBLISHERS & DISTRIBUTORS (P) LTD

7/22, Ansari Road, Darya Ganj, New Delhi-110002
Phones : +91-11-40775252, 40775214, 23273880, 23275880
Fax : +91-11-23285873
Web : www.atlanticbooks.com
E-mail : orders@atlanticbooks.com

Branch Office: Chennai
Phones : +91-44-48531784, 28291383
E-mail : chennai@atlanticbooks.com

Reprint 2020

Printed & bound in India by Atlantic Print Services

Dedicated to

My brother

Ravi Prakash Pradhan

Acknowledgements

I take this opportunity to thank all those people who have directly or indirectly helped me in bringing out this book in such a nice form. I am extremely thankful to my learned professors Dr. A.N. Dwivedi, Dr. Rajnath, Dr. R.K. Shukla and Dr. R.N. Rai for their constant encouragement to complete the book. I am deeply indebted to my father Dr. R.P. Pradhan, former Reader & Head, Dept. of English, P.G. College, Ghazipur, who has been a source of academic inspiration to me. I shall be ungrateful if I do not make mention of my mother Smt. Champa Rai, whose motherly care and support enabled me to accomplish this task. I acknowledge with thanks my wife Chandralekha Rai's cooperation, encouragement and concern ceaselessly shown during the period of editing this book. I also appreciate the cooperation of my sons—Yash and Harsh. Special thanks are also due to V.N. Rai (I.P.S.), Manoj Sinha (former Member of Parliament) and Mrs. Tanu Rai for their valuable advice received from time to time.

R.P. Pradhan

Preface

The book, comprising nineteen papers on diverse subjects, contributed by erudite scholars, seeks to present contemporary consciousness and sensibility through the literary genre of poetry, fiction and criticism. In the first section, three poets, who have assimilated various cultural experiences on global level, have been included. Anne Sexton in her twin themes of love and death is highly self-revealing in her poems. *I Hold Back Nothing* may be taken as the motto of her poetry. She does not suppress facts about herself and in that way she may earn the title of a confessional poetess. Her act of self-revelation without any reservations is a typical modern trait.

The other poetess, Imtiaz Dharker, with her multi-cultural experiences of Pakistan, Britain and India, dwells upon man-woman relationship in which forces of disintegration are often at work but her poems serve as a kind of bridge. Ramanujan's religious sentiments along with social and secular sensibilities, have also been recorded because they place Indian English poetry on a universal level.

In the second section, which is comprised of fictional literature, the common themes presented are the issues of diaspora; the problems of self-discovery; the search for identity; the factors of race and gender causing conjugal disharmony; marital disputes; depraved condition of immigrant women; and general feeling of isolation, frustration and depression. The question of identity appears at *The Impressionist*. Pran Nath, the illegitimate child of Amrita and British Ronald Forester is born after Amrita's marriage with Pandit Amarnath. When Pran Nath is fifteen years old, Pandit dies but before his death he comes to learn the true parentage of Pran Nath and turns the boy out of his house. There starts the process of self-discovery for Pran Nath. He moves from place to place and from identity to identity. The novelist seems to conclude that identity as a concept cannot be basic, invariable and pre-social.

Toni Morrison, an Afro-American novelist, studies in her novel *The Bluest Eye* the same problem of identity. Pecola's overvaluation of white beauty causes in her a feeling of self-hatred and it brings about her tragedy. The black girl wants to follow the white model of beauty. She aspires to possess blue eyes and in that way she is mocked and condemned by both the classes of the Black and the White. She stands "nowhere" and is segregated from society. She is made the scapegoat.

Kamala Markandaya, a pioneer of the Indian diaspora, shows in her novel *The Nowhere Man* the confrontation between the East and the West. She introduces the issues of races, cultures and modes of living. She balances the Oriental and Occidental values of life.

Bharati Mukherjee in *The World According to Hsü* interrogates Canadian multiculturalism from the viewpoints of diaspora. Ratna Clayton, who is half European and half Indian, is excluded from the stream of Canadian life because of her dark skin. She faces the problem of cultural identity. Her other novel *Jasmine* also presents an immigrant woman's position. It is a quest for identity in an alien land. It is the story of a young widow who uproots herself from her life in India and goes to America in search of a new life. There she kills the captain of a ship after being raped by him. In this world she finds only despair and loss. She faces obstacles one after another. She is caught between Eastern and Western world and cannot feel at home anywhere.

Shashi Deshpande in *The Dark Holds No Terrors* explores the myth of man's superiority and the suppression of a career woman. Sarita, a successful doctor in the day time, becomes a "terrified trapped animal" at night in the grip of her sadist husband. After fifteen years, she returns to her father's house to escape from the brutality of her husband inflicted on her every night.

Nobel laureate Jelinek portrays in her works the wretched condition of the fairer sex under the male domination. Most of her heroines appear as objects of sexual gratification for the male society. Jelinek has been badly criticized in America for writing pornography but the truth is that she is a novelist and not a moral philosopher. Her presentation is realistic.

Further, Jhumpa Lahiri has accurately diagnosed the maladies of Indian immigrants with particular reference to women. The woman enters the "host" country which appears at first to be a promised land for her but there she battles adversity—both mental and material. She becomes an exile or rather a slave transported across an ocean.

The Inheritance of Loss records painful experiences of Biju who happens to be an illegal immigrant.

Bapsi Sidhwa's *Ice-Candy Man*, in spite of its political leanings, shows the human condition in which a woman is often marginalized. It has been written with a feminist outlook which shows woman's secondary status in society.

In the third section, essays related to the literary theories of postmodernism, postcolonialism and deconstruction have been studied. They may help us in the understanding of most of the works which have been written in these perspectives.

This book will be highly useful to the students, teachers and researchers of English literature in general and those interested in contemporary English literature in particular.

R.P. Pradhan

Contents

Poetry

I Hold Back Nothing: Anne Sexton's Preoccupations with Love and Death

1

A.N. Dwivedi

One of the foremost qualities of a Confessional poet is the baring of his/her heart to readers, without concealing anything about himself/herself, and this quality is amply found in Anne Sexton. As a poet, she does not suppress facts about herself and her experiences of life. This is how she endears herself to her readers who feel all along that they are perfectly trusted by the writer and not cheated with vague generalisations or unfelt thoughts of a dreamer. Anne Sexton is highly self-revealing in her poems of Love and Death, and her act of self-revelation, without any reservations, at once puts her in the category of Confessional poets. Initially, she resisted the efforts of critics to brand her a Confessional poet, but later she got reconciled to it and remarked as follows: 'For years I railed against being put in this category...then about a year ago, I decided I was the only confessional poet. Well...Allen Ginsberg too. He holds back nothing and I hold back nothing'. Well, 'I hold back nothing' may be taken as the motto of Sexton's poetry. Right from her first collection of poem, *To Bedlam and Part Way Back* (1960) to *The Awful Rowing Towards God* (1975), she has surprised her readers with her shocking realistic details. The epigraph attached to her second book of poetry, *All My Pretty Ones* makes it quite clear; here she states that '...a book should serve as the axe for the frozen sea within us'.

I

Anne Sexton treats the theme of Love on a wide canvas, touching upon almost all its shades—joy in fulfilment, sorrow in separation; love sensual, filial, adulterous; love of self and impossibility of reciprocal love. Sexton's books 'read like a fever chart for a bad case of melancholy', and through them she sought to release her tension caused by religion, drugs, suicide attempts, art, and lovers. Of all these matters, love and mourning (due to non-fulfilment of her desire) constitute the most dominant themes in her poetry.

Sexton considers Love as a close companion of Sorrow or Death. The first volume of her poetry, *To Bedlam and Part Way Back* (1960), contains a poem called "The Moss of His Skin", structurally a dramatic monologue, which attempts a psychoanalytical probe into the female feeling of guilt at the sharing of the father along with the mother. This poem is quoted below at some length:

> It was only important
> to smile and hold still,
> to lie down beside him
> and to rest awhile,
> to be folded up together
> as if we were silk,
> to sink from the eyes of mother
> and not to talk.
>
> The black room took us
> like a cave or a mouth
> or an indoor belly.
>
> I held my breath
> and daddy was there,
>
> ... ...
>
> I lay by the moss
> of his skin until
> it grew strange. My sisters
> will never know that I fall
> out of myself and pretend
> that Allah will not see
> how I hold my daddy
> like an old stone tree.

With the help of four grave figures (or images), the poetess tries to establish her feeling of guilt—those of 'the black room' (the place of committing sin), 'a cave' (privacy), 'a mouth' (self-annihilation), and 'an indoor belly' (the complex female need)—

which requires punishment. This feeling of guilt is, in fact, more severe than that of Antigone's, but it is also more natural for an adult woman.

Another poem, "Where I Live in This Honorable House of the Laurel Tree", details an 'erotic paralysis' that results from refusing courtship:

... The air
rings for you, for that astonishing rite
of my breathing tent undone within your Right.

I only know how this untimely last has tossed
flesh at the wind forever and moved my fears
toward the intimate Rome of the myth we crossed.

The courtship offers a divine occasion for the two loving hearts to come together and understand each other but the beloved has her own 'fears' and she turns it down.

The poem which has caused great confusion among critics and scholars is "Unknown Girl in the Maternity Ward". Here the girl having given birth to the child tells the latter that—

... Your lips are animals, you are fed
with love. At first hunger is not wrong.

This poem gave rise to the speculation whether or not Anne Sexton had had an illegitimate child, but this speculation amused even the poetess. What is of greater importance in the poem is "the experience of childbirth with its essential pain of separation".[1] People of discerning talent have almost always identified childbirth with pain-making; and Sexton does the same here. In this context, it is pertinent to recall another poem "For Johnny Pole on the Forgotten Beach", which also informs us that "He [Johnny] was my brother, my small Johnny brother, almost ten," and that he was killed on a 'beach of assault' in war. The truth, however, is that Sexton herself clarified to an interviewer that she had no brother as such who was killed during the war. Very often, she rather assumed the role of the persona, speaking through another's mouth.

"The Bells" evokes the image of an ironic paradise lost, and though it is quite free of 'narcissim', it *does* display 'the knowledge of the serpent in paradise.' A strong sense of eroticism, similar to that of "When I Live", is to be had in this poetic piece. Mark the following lines in this connection:

Oh see the naughty clown
and the wild parade
while love love
love grew rings around me.

This was the sound when it began;
our breath pounding up to see
the flying man breast out
across the boarded sky
and climb the air.

I remember the color of music
and how forever
all the trembling bells of you
were mine.

In a diction of understatement here, Sexton makes the question of courtship, one of the most memorable infernal events, reducing the divine lover, Apollo, of "When I Live" to the childlike 'flying man'. Obviously, Sexton becomes naughty in this place.

As stated earlier, the poems in the first volume dealing with the theme of love clearly go with a tortuous sense of guilt and mourning. The second volume of Sexton's poetry also carries a similar treatment of love. The title-piece, "All My Pretty Ones", is taken from Macduff's speech in Shakespeare's *Macbeth*, and reinforces the idea of sinfulness that grips the speaker-persona at the loss of the loved ones.

In the second volume, we love a poem entitled "The Truth the Dead Know", which is headed by a dedication:

For my mother, born March 1902, died March 1959
and my father, born February 1900, died June 1959.

This poem is manifestly a refusal to mourn and a reaffirmation of indulgence in physical love:

    In another country people die.
My darling, the wind falls in like stones
from the whitehearted water and when we touch

we enter touch entirely. No one's alone.
Men kill for this, or for as much.

From the above-quoted lines, it is clear that Sexton does not want to grieve over the departed ones; instead, she wants to pass her days in love-making, which alone can remove her loneliness and boredom. But in the poem "The Fortress", which is addressed to Sexton's daughter, Linda, the poetess gives vent to a different kind of feeling —very tender and motherly and consolatory:

We laugh and touch.
I promise you love. Time will not take away that....

Here the poetess's love for her daughter is deep and unshakable.

The other poems in the second volume mostly treat the subject of mourning and death. But the last poem, "Dearest", strives to reach consolation through religion and love—the two bedrocks of family relationships. Though this poem also mentions death, it ends on a note of reconciliation with the inevitable:

Dearest,
where are your letters?
The madman is an impostor.
He is actually my grandfather.
He floats far off in the storm
with his nicotine mustache and a bagful of nickels.
His legs stumble through
baskets of eyelashes.

Now he is gone
as you are gone.
But he belongs to me like lost baggage.

In fact, the poem has "the nostalgia for and denial of absolute love."[2]

Sexton's third book of poetry, *Live or Die* (1966), won the Pulitzer Prize for her. It definitely marks a transition from her previous work—"a passage from pessimism to optimism".[3] The poems contained in it are chronologically arranged and bring out the poet's inner and outer lives during January 1962-February 1966. This poetical volume begins with an account of her father's death—the father with whom she had reached a reconciliation of sorts just before his death. Taken as a whole, it is riddled with guilt, with feeling of sin towards her mother as well as towards her daughter.

Sexton's treatment of love reaches its climax in the next volume called *Love Poems* (1967), which probes into sensual, filial, impious, and personal kinds of love in one place. Most of these love poems underline the feelings of disappointment and hopelessness in reciprocal love, and a number of them depict her struggle against loneliness and frustration. The opening poem of the volume, "The Touch" is particularly poignant. There are two poems in it — "December 9th" and "The Papa and Mama Dance" —which fall beyond the pale of love poetry and appear to be antiwar pieces. But there is a whole cluster of poems which recounts the various conditions of womankind: "In Celebration of My Uterus", "The Nude Surin", "Song for a Red Night Gown", "Loving the Killer", and "December 18th". This volume concludes with a sequence of eighteen short poems under the caption "Eighteen Days Without You". In these poems, Sexton tries to superimpose her "surreal dream imagery upon the no less horrifying realities of modern life."[4]

The next volume, *Transformations* (1971), is a rich collection of seventeen long poems, which deal more with allegory and mythology than with treatment of love or religion. They are verily the fairy tales told by Grimm and transformed into grim parables of our time. The old and the new meet here, and in the words of Kurt Vonnegut, Jr., Anne Sexton is "telling many of Grimm's fairy tales in poetry."[5] In this volume, "Cinderella" is a very outstanding poetic tale.

In *The Book of Folly* (1972), the themes of Love and Death become predominant. Consisting of 30 poems in all, 3 stories and 9 Jesus papers, the volume becomes interesting for its two groups of poems known as "The Death of the Fathers" and "Angels of the Love-Affair". In the poem "Mother and Daughter," the mother says to her daughter thus:

Now that you are eighteen
I give you my booty, my spoils,
my Mother & Co., and my ailments.

> Question you about this
> and you'll not know the answer —

Another poem, "The Wifebeater", presents a dismal and dreary picture of the domestic life, and the poet writes thus:

> Tonight all the red dogs be down in fear
> and the wife and daughter knit into each other
> until they are killed.

Unlike Judith Wright, the celebrated Australian poetess who is no less 'confessional' than Anne or Sylvia, the poet rebels against Man as a whole and his traditional role of superiority in any way. In the poem "The Assassin", she says thus:

> I know his male 'sex' and I do
> march over him with my index finger.
>
> His mouth and his anus are one.
> I'm at the center of feeling.

Her avowed hatred for the malekind is also vented in the poem "Begot", the sixth piece in "The Death of the Fathers":

> Stranger,
> stranger,
> take away your riddle.
>
> Give it to a medical school
> for I sicken.
>
> My loss knocks.

Explicitly, Sexton is fed up with the proud boast of the male ego as well as with his sex-dominated approaches to her. She is, therefore, 'sick' with a thought of him and does not want him near her any longer.

The poems contained in "Angels of the Love Affair" are very tense and powerful. These poems are: (1) Angel of Fire and Genitals, (2) Angel of Clean Sheets, (3) Angel of Flight and Sleigh Bells, (4) Angel of Hope and Calendars, (5) Angel of Blizzards and Blackouts, and (6) Angel of Beach Houses and Picnics. The first-named poem celebrates the Angel of Fire and Genitals as a Mother, who is bubbling with energy and absorption of an unusual nature:

> Mother of fire, let me stand at your devouring gate

as the sun dies in your arms and you loosen its
terrible weight.

The Angel, no doubt, represents Motherhood at her best; she may sacrifice herself but in the interest of 'the sun', which is a symbol of male energy, the discharge of which through her lessens his burden.

As in the Jesus papers, so in the volume *The Awful Rowing Towards God* (1975), we do not find anything worthwhile about Love and Death. The poems in it are rather intended as powerful satires of Christ. If someone asks: "Would you mock God?" To which the poet replies: "God is not mocked except by believers" (Jesus Paper I). *The Awful Rowing* is though not as satirical and biting as the Jesus Papers, it is an 'awful' (as the title indicates) experience all the same.

The next volume consisting of 114 pages, *45 Mercy Street* (1976), charts out Sexton's "poetic growth and the events of her life from 1971 through 1974,"[6] as her own daughter informs us. In this volume, we have a poem entitled "Killing the Love", which is laved in dreadful feelings of dejection and anger at love's unfulfilment:

I am the love killer,
I am murdering the music we thought so special;
that blazed between us, over and over.

I am murdering me, where I kneeled at your kiss.
I am pulsing knives through the hands
that created two into one.

Sexton is decidedly not happy with conjugal love that demands frequent knockings at its gate. So was Sylvia Plath, and so possibly will be all hypersensitive women. And if Love is not to be realised, Death can be.

II

Death becomes a complement to Love, a fulfilment of the unrequited desire, in the hands of Anne Sexton. Here all the anxious worms of love are subsumed; here all the pricks and pains of the ungrateful, selfish human world disappear. This is what we discover in her autobiographical poems right from the first volume to the last.

"You, Doctor Martin," the first poem in the first volume, refers to a mental hospital as a 'summer hotel' where the dance of Death is clearly visible:

> You, Doctor Martin, walk
> from breakfast to madness. Late August,
> I speed through the antiseptic tunnel
> where the moving dead still talk
> of pushing their bones against the thrust
> of cure. And I am queen of this summer hotel
> or the laughing bee on a stalk
> of death.

This passage follows the Dantean image of the dead who do not know they are in hell, and in "the laughing bee on a stalk" it has a sexual image, which suggests pollination.[7] The death-image is definitely dominant herein.

"The Double Image" running into five sections and addressed to the poet's second daughter, Joyce, plays up the death theme by reminiscing the mother who is long dead:

> You call me *mother* and I remember my mother again,
> somewhere in greater Boston, dying.

The whole poem reads like a personal history of the poetess, and the happy home-scene cannot keep off the portrait of the dead mother.

Both the title and the epigraph to *All My Pretty Ones* highlight an unsavoury and a bit shocking mourning over death. The title takes us to Shakespeare's *Macbeth* where Macduff is terribly upset at the horrible news of his children's ghastly assassination:

> All my pretty ones?
> Did you say all? Oh hell-kite ! All?
> What? all my pretty chickens and their dam
> At one fell swoop? ...

and the epigraph, a citation from a letter of Franz Kafka to Oskar Pollak, reads like this— '...a book should serve as the axe for the frozen sea within us'. In this book, the poem "The Truth the Dead Know" underlines the value of love in the face of death:

And what of the dead? They lie without shoes
in their stone boats. They are more like stone
than the sea would be if it stopped. They refuse
to be blessed, throat, eye and knucklebone.

This poem reinforces the idea of nothingness, annihilation, and refusal 'to be blessed'.

There are some poems in this book which bring out the poet's religious longings *vis-à-vis* 'the terrible ordinariness of Christ's suffering on the cross'; for example "For God While Sleeping" and "In the Deep Museum". Even the title-piece "All My Pretty Ones" treats the dead father as a God:

My God, father, each Christmas day
with your blood, will I drink down your glass
of wine?

And the closing poem "Dearest" combines love and death in its texture, beginning with a reference to the dead:

It is snowing, grotesquely snowing,
upon the small faces of the dead.
Those dear loudmouths, gone for over a year,
buried side by side
like little wrens.

The imagery is quite arresting here, comparing 'the small faces' with 'little wrens.'

The third volume of Sexton's poetry, *Live or Die* (1966), juxtaposes life and death, and the title also suggests it. Here the poetess is concerned with the limits of the body and its failure to rise to the occasion and meet its demands. This volume opens with the direct description of her father's death.

The Book of Folly (1972) also contains a distinct group of six poems entitled "The Death of the Fathers" which unmistakably deal with the theme of death. The third poem in this group, "The Firebombers", creates an atmosphere of horror and death from the very start:

We are America.
We are the coffin fillers.
We are the grocers of death.
We pack them in crates like cauliflowers.

The fifth poem, "The Silence", equates 'silence' with 'death' in unequivocal terms. In this book, the Jesus Papers are full of references to Christ's unusual suffering and crucifixion.

The religious feelings surge up in *The Awful Rowing Towards God,* but even here the poet does not forget to mention her sickness leading to the dream of death. In the poem "The Sickness Unto Death", Sexton writes:

> My kindred, my brother, I said
> and gave the yellow daisy
> to the crazy woman in the next bed.

Explicitly, 'the yellow daisy' is a symbol of death, recalling the dire moment of the grave.

The most typical poem of Sexton is "Killing the Love", where the twin subjects of Love and Death jostle with each other. And when love is no more a prop for her and she turns out to be a 'love killer', she consorts with 'the dead':

> Now I am alone with the dead,
> flying off bridges,
> hurling myself like a beer can into the wastebasket.
>
> ....
>
> though I fly and hurl,
> my insides are empty
> and my face is as blank as a wall.

She is unquestionably totally hopeless and 'blank' in her life, and so she prefers death to death-in-life.

III

Sexton as a poet is inescapably preoccupied with the twin themes of Love and Death. Other themes, such as religion and God and the self, are not so insistent in her poetry. Like the Metaphysical poets, especially John Donne, Sexton also takes love and death as the two sides of the same coin, though she differs from them in that she does not make 'death' a metaphor of 'love'. For her, they remain two distinct 'sides', supplementing each other in moments of need. When one fails to serve her need, she goes in for the other, without fear or hesitation. And in the handling of these two themes, Sexton does not conceal anything; she rather candidly reveals the various shades of love and death in her poetry.

REFERENCES

1. Beverly Fields, "The Poetry of Anne Sexton", *Poets in Progress*, ed. Edward Hungerford (Northwestern University, U.S.A.: Northwestern University Press, 1967), p. 257.
2. *Ibid.*, p. 284.
3. Robert Phillips, *The Confessional Poets* (Carbondale & Edwardsville: Southern Illinois University Press, 1973), p. 30.
4. *Ibid.*, p. 88.
5. Kurt Vonnegut, Jr., "Preface", *Transformations* (Boston: Houghton Mifflin Co., 1971), p. ix.
6. Linda Gray Sexton, "Note", *45 Mercy Street* (Boston: Houghton Mifflin Co., 1976), p. vii.
7. Beverly Fields, *loc. cit.*, p. 268.

Edgy Counters: The Poetry of Imtiaz Dharker

2

K.M. Pandey

Imtiaz Dharker is a well-known name in Indian English Poetry. Her two volumes *Purdah and Other Poems* (1988) and *Postcards from God* (1994) introduce a considerably different world in which one notices a kind of warfare which has been termed "edgy counters" in the present paper. She has multicultural experiences of specially three countries — Pakistan, Britain and India. She was born in a Muslim family in Lahore, grew up in Glasgow and now lives in Mumbai. Married to a Hindu but following her own religion, she now lives in her adopted country, India. In an interview to Eunice de Souza, she talks about freedom, alienation and outsiderness, "Freedom is something inside you. Being able to stand outside a culture is freedom. I love being an outsider. I'd say 'alienation', being an outsider is a positive. Not alienated really, but outside. Being an outsider is my country. I value that. That's the country all writers belong to — standing outside the body too, outside the image. Inside we are so many different things" (Eunice de Souza, 2002: 114).

The poems in *Purdah* are about being a woman and not just a Muslim woman. She does not see herself as the spokesperson for the community. "Her poetry is consciously feminist, consciously political, consciously that of a multiple outsider, someone who knows her own mind, rather than someone full of doubt and liberal ironies." (King, 2001:321) Argumentative and dramatic in structure, her poems acquire a kind of universality. The title poem begins with the poetess' observation of the social mores which condition the growing girl:

One day they said
she was old enough to learn some shame.
She found it came quite naturally.

It is the beginning of 'purdah' for the growing girl and Dharker sees it as a metaphor for shell and safety:

Purdah is a kind of safety.
The body finds a place to hide.
The cloth fans out against the skin
much like the earth that falls
on coffins after they put the dead men in.

(p. 3)

But purdah is a kind of distancing of the self from the world. To reach the growing girl's psyche, the poet keeps on opening the doors "inward and again/inward" (p. 4) "Purdah II" is a series of unveiling the veils of several women growing, young and old. This the new Hajii, just fifteen, snaps a flower off his garland and looks at the girl and drops a flower on her Book:

There was nothing holy in his look.
Hands that had prayed at Mecca
dropped a sly flower on your book
and the girl's breasts, still tiny, grow an inch.

(p. 6)

These girls sold and bought, are "unwilling virgins who has been taught, / especially in this strangers' land, to bind / their brightness tightly round, / whatever they might wear, / in the purdah of the mind". (p. 7) The poet persona makes it clear that the same fate has been written by the society for many other women:

There are so many of me.
I have met them, meet them everyday,
recognise their shadows on the streets.
I know their past and future
in the cautious way they place their feet.

(p. 8)

The same fate awaits the women of different groups and the poetess feels the need of breaking the cover that binds the women:

Break cover
Break cover and let us see
the ghosts of the girls with tell-tale lips.

(p. 9)

The four sections of Purdah — Purdah, the Haunted House, The Child Sings, and Borderlines — move around the basic questions of freedom for females in male-oriented world. K. Satchidanandan sees double marginalisation in these poems. Thus "the purdah that keeps her hidden from the world forces her to travel into the inner world: hers is also an experience of double marginalisation: first as a member of a minority community, then marginalised by that community's patriarchy." (2003:20).

The man-woman relationship, in which the woman is at a loss is the theme of "No-Man's Land" in "Borderlines — Battlefields I":

It is the women who know
you can take in
the invader, time after time,
and still be whole.

(p. 51)

The obvious sensual overtone suggests the kind of change that the poet expects for her poetic persona. Referring to this role of the poet, Annamma Jeseph observes:

> Dharker's preoccupation is with social change. She does not get emotionally involved with the victim. It is as if she is outside the circus ring where defenceless human beings are bought to their heels by the active evil working through patriarchal oppression and dehumisation. She is the thinking, feeling human being, flustered by her helplessness and ineffectiveness, trying to use the power of the world against satanic forces.
>
> (Joseph, 2000:116)

The edgy counters take a wider spectrum in the second volume, *Postcards from God* (1994). The volume has three main sections, Postcards from God, Naming the Angels, and Bombay: The Name of God. Most of these poems are juxtaposed with Dharker's own drawings which are of two types: "first, finely pencilled faces in close-up drawn as studies in ramshackle ordinariness, just this side of the grotesque, often with superimposed reticulations, as of bars or grilles; and second, views either of old buildings, or their interiors, or views glimpsed out of their windows, again with superimposed grids, like bars" (Patke, 2003:271).

The title *Postcards from God* is ironic and in many of these poems, the poet persona is God Himself who comes to this world as a visitor to find that nobody recognises Him in the places meant for Him:

> Here, in this strange place,
> in a disjointed time,
> I am nothing but a space
> that someone has to fill.
>
> Images invade me
> Picture postcards overlap my empty face,
> demanding to be stamped and sent.
>
> (p. 3)

This makes Him ask few questions. In "Question 1" He asks why He cannot hear His people:

> I have the biggest remote control
> of all. I can channel-hop
> and skip and jump
> across the world, turning your voices
> on and off, start and rewind,
> play and stop,
> fast forward squeak and double-speak,
> murmur mutter mute stammer stutter
> gabble rattle rap rasp shout croak
> shriek whisper scream chant sing. Nothing.
> Static. Snow. White nose.
> You're off the air.
>
> Am I there
> When I can't hear your voice ?
>
> (p. 30)

The long list of mechanical sounds does not reach Him. This leads Him to think that perhaps He is in the silence — when human beings remain in their selves. The second question, "Question 2", reverts the myth that God created human beings in His own image. He is puzzled whether He created human beings or human beings created Him:

Did I create you
in my image
or did you create me
in yours ?

(p. 32)

It is worthwhile to remind ourselves that the whole volume has its origin in the incident of the demolition of the old Ramjanmabhumi temple-cum-mosque that took place in Ayodhya on 6 December, 1992 and the communal carnage that took place in several parts of the country, the more so in Bombay. Talking to Eunice de Souza, Dharker said:

> Two things were happening. Post-Babri Masjid, I felt the whole situation was very fragile. I was also looking at images of almost collapsing structures, buildings propped up, which extended to faith being propped up, and human survival. The bewilderment of humans was transposed to the God persona.
>
> (de Souza, 2002:115)

The general discussion becomes more specific in terms of place and atmosphere in the remaining two sections of the volume. Many poems of section II, "Naming the Angels", move in and around Dharavi, the largest slum in Asia. The poem "Making the Angels" is built up on the mythopoeic imagination that gods were made out of grapes and demons out of rock: "A host of fledgling angels, spat/ like grape-seed, out/ of a newmade, unsuspecting sky." "Naming the Angels" connotes the basic sin of pride: "Alone, within /the pride of being named —/ the first sin."

The poem "Namesake" is written on the ten year old Adam who is the brother of Zarina, the girl who was looked after by the poet as a member of the UNICEF team. The poet says that except for the namesake there is no similarity between this Adam and the mythical, biblical Adam:

Adam, your namesake lives
in Dharavi, ten years old. He
has never faced the angels, survives
with pigs that root
outside the door,
gets up at four,
follows his mother to the hotel
where he helps her cut
the meat and vegetables, washes
it all well, watches
the pots over the stove
and waits, his eyelids drooping,
while behind the wall she sells herself
as often as she can before
they have to hurry home.

(p. 64)

This Adam does not have any memory of the Garden of Eden or the Tree of Knowledge:

He never turns to look at you.
He has no memory
of the Garden, paradise water
or the Tree.

(p. 64)

In the other poem, "Adam from New Zealand", Adam is a twenty-six year old journalist from New Zealand who wants to have first-hand knowledge of Dharavi in Bombay and through it the whole country:

So on his way into Bombay
he has decided he must see
the real India in Dharavi.

He wants a guided tour,
to be fitted in his schedule
between the film studio
and a visit to the Chor Bazaar.

(p. 69)

But the poet refuses to take him to the place where Zarina lives because Adam wants to use his cameras, microphones, sunguns, recorders and dictaphones and these random cameras will swallow up the souls of those who reside there:

> How can I serve up Zarina
> or her brother Adam
> to their random cameras ?
>
> They will smile shyly.
>
> The aperture will open
> to swallow up their souls.
>
> (p. 69)

The poet knows that the mother of Zarina and Adam will greet them with Thums Up or glasses of sweet tea and will put on her brave face but everyone in Dharavi will know that the world has come to make a side-show of her poverty. She knows that they will not come to make a record of Zarina's wedding or a video of Adam's bride ten years later. So, she is firm on keeping him away from the greedy camera because "He is too precious for you to see."

The poems of the last section, "Bombay: The Name of God", are more specific and personal. The first poem, "Seats of Power", takes into account the required formalities for carnage in the city in the wake of the demolition of the Babri Masjid:

> Speeches are read.
>
> A few points made.
>
> Somewhere else in the city
> a blade finds flesh.
>
> Here, in this quiet, civil room
> permission has been given
> for the carnage to begin.
>
> (p. 78)

It is a committed political poetry in the wake of communal carnage. Thus in the "6 December 1992" she satirises those political leaders who are involved in such activities:

> Glass leaders laugh
> and the whole world can see
> right through their faces
> into their black tongues.
>
> (p. 79)

The poem "8 January 1993" captures the scene of destruction after a series of bomb blasts in which a large number of people were killed brutally:

> The bolt bangs in.
> A match is struck and thrown.
> The burning has begun.
>
> Afterwards
> the bodies are removed
> one by one.
>
> And this is left:
> blackened sarees, trousers, petticoats
> the shell of a television set,
> a tin box of bangles
> and face cream,
> a blistered cupboard
> like a looted face
> that opened its mouth
>
> in a scream
> that never found an end.

(p. 81)

The poem "The Name of God" juxtaposes the two different ways in which the name of God was uttered. There were those who were killing people in the name of God and also the poet persona who runs away with her daughter taking the name of God:

> The name of god
> in my mouth
> had a taste I soon forgot.
> I think it was the taste
> of home.

(p. 84)

The poem entitled "The List" suggests the disintegration of the city in the wake of violence:

> Sudden impact
> The city flies apart.

Bits of high-rise apartments,
scraps of slums,
all kinds of shops
empty themselves into the sky.

Loaves of bread explode from bakeries.
Fishes catapult out of the sea.
Bushes, suburban trains and taxies
spit out their load.
Things lose their names.

(p. 92)

But for the comment of Dharker one would take these images to be arising from the bomb blasts in Bombay. She says, "Most people think these images came from the bomb blasts, but in fact I read the poem at Horniman Circle a month before the blasts. The images were of a city disintegrating" (de Souza, 2002:117). The disintegration takes place in the name of communal animosity, so the poet says:

Your name is there.
It settles on you like a shroud.

(p. 93)

The poem "Untitled" brings about the poet's relationship with the city. She says that she does not live in the city; rather she collides with the city and in this collision both she and the city have survived:

I wouldn't say I live in this city.
Everyday it comes
and collides with me.

I had begun to see
that this daily accident
had its funny side.
Years after I arrived
and after several attempts to leave
I decided to unpack my bags.

The city and I had both survived.
or so we thought.

(p. 98)

One morning, the poet takes the breath of the city air and realises that both she as well as her city were going to die. It is not abstraction but reality:

It's not Bombay that burns,
but this specific child
screaming behind a bolted door ;
this particular man on fire
trapped inside his locked car.

(p. 98)

These scenes make the poet feel her spiritual death. She wishes such harsh reality to be imaginary but it is a reality that finds place in the poem:

I wish these were imagined things.
I wish I could put them
safely in another poem.
reconcile them with this
paper and this pen
so I could never smell the burning
or hear the breaking glass again.

(p. 99)

"This," says Bruce King (2001:325), "is committed poetry, committed to the politics of truth and humanity rather than party or ideology".

The last poem "Minority" suggests what her poems intend to do. They have the capacity to fight back and so they have their relevance. They can make the reader recognise someone's face as her or his:

until, one day, you meet
the stranger sidling down your street,
realize you know the face
simplified to bone,
look into its outcast eyes
and recognize it as your own.

(p. 103)

Thus, the image of the world that emerges from the poems of Dharker is that of a disintegrating one. The poet succeeds in representing the edgy counters between the male-female world as well as the majority-minority nexus. The poems seem to be a kind of bridge between such forces of disintegration. They also signify the hope that lies with the world as well as its inhabitants.

WORKS CITED

de Souza, Eunice. ed. *Nine Indian Women Poets: An Anthology*. 1997. New Delhi: OUP, 2001.

—. ed. *Talking Poems: Conversations With Poets*. 1999. New Delhi: OUP, 2002.

Dharker, Imtiaz. *Purdah and Other Poems*. Delhi: OUP, 1988.

—.*Postcards from God*. New Delhi: Viking, 1994.

Joseph, Annamma. "The Metamorphosis of the Pardah: Imtiaz Dharker". *Modern Indian Poetry in English: Critical Studies*, ed. Shah and Nayar. New Delhi: Creative Books, 2002.

King, Bruce. *Modern Indian Poetry in English*. 1987. New Delhi. OUP revised edition, 2001.

Naik, M.K. and Narayan Shymala. *Indian English Literature 1980-2000: A Critical Survey*. New Delhi: Pencraft International, 2001.

Patke, Rajeev S. "Poetry Since Independence". *An Illustrated History of Indian Literature in English*, ed. A. K. Mehrotra. Delhi: Permanent Black, 2003.

Satchinandan, K. "Alternative Nationhoods in Contemporary Indian Poetry". *Authors Texts, Issues: Essays on Indian Literature*. Delhi: Pencraft International, 2003.

Sen, Sudeep. "Midnights [Grand] Children: Post-Independence Indian Poetry in English". *Trends and Techniques in Contemporary Indian English Poetry*, ed. Rama Nair. New Delhi: Prestige Books, 2001.

Treatment of Hindu Mythology in Ramanujan's *Second Sight* and *The Black Hen*

3

Anju Mishra

A.K. Ramanujan (1929-93), who has produced four volumes of poetry to this day— *The Striders* (1966), *Relations* (1971), *Second Sight* (1986), and *The Black Hen* (1995), is a distinctive name in contemporary Indian English poetry. He is usually bracketed with Nissim Ezekiel, Dom Moraes, Kamala Das and K.N. Daruwalla in point of popularity, but the quality of his verse— his tense and taut diction, his complex style, his modernistic approach to life, his tone of disillusionment, his witty remarks, and his deep-rootedness in Hindu myths and legends— immediately places him head and shoulder above many other Indian poets of today. Here in this paper, I shall examine the use of Hindu mythology in the last two volumes of Ramanujan.

Second Sight is sufficiently rich in the depiction of Hindu myths and legends, gods and goddesses, even the Indian ways of life. In this poetical collection, we have a poem titled "No Amnesiac King", which records the popular legend of King Dusyanta and forest-beauty Shakuntala (who was the adopted daughter of Rishi Kanva). They had wedded in the thick forest by taking to the Gandharva system of marriage, and the King had gifted her a glittering ring. After spending some time with her, the king returned to his kingdom and forgot all about her. A few months later, Shakuntala left for her husband's abode in a state of expectancy. On the way, she took bath in a river. She then came to the court where she was not recognised by the King. The reason for this was that she had lost the wedding ring gifted to her by him while she was taking her bath in the river. The ring was swallowed up by a fish which was later caught by fishermen and handed over to the royal cook who cut it open and surprisingly discovered the ring in its belly. Getting back the ring, the King recovered all his lost memory. Mark, how well this ancient tale has been retold by Ramanujan:

One cannot wait any more in the back
of one's mind for that conspiracy

of three fishermen and a palace cook
to bring, dressed in cardamom and clove,

the one well-timed memorable fish,
so one can cut straight with the royal knife

to the ring waiting in the belly,
and recover at one stroke all lost memory....[1]

The poet calls it "a forest/legend of wandering king and waiting/innocent, complete with fawn under tree/and inverse images in the water / of a stream that runs as if it doesn't" (p.17). Afterwards in the poem, Ramanujan reverts to his own wife in a swift transition of thought and suggests that he cannot forget about her even for a while when she goes to the market place to buy fish from the fisherman in the full gaze of all. He also suggests that in such matters even a common man is much better than a king like Dusyanta. Thus, an old legend is wonderfully presented to us with a modernistic touch.

Another poem employing mythopoeic form for its enrichment is "A Minor Sacrifice" in five parts. The very opening of the poem introduces the old story of Raja Parikshit and his son Janmejaya. The poet writes thus:

I'd just heard that day
of the mischievous king in the epic
who kills a snake in the forest
and thinks it would be such fun
to garland a sage's neck
with the old dead thing,
and so he does,
and promptly earns a curse,
an early death by snakebite.

His son vows vengeance
and performs a sacrifice,
a magic rite
that draws every snake from everywhere,
till snakes of every stripe
begin to fall
through the blazing air
into his altar fires.

(p. 35)

The quoted passage clearly narrates the legend of killing a snake by Raja Parikshit, who was now in the terrible grip of *Kaliyuga* having taken his seat in his golden crown in a deep forest while on a hunting spree, and garlanding it around the neck of a sage called Shringi. This unwarranted action of the King, immediately invited the wrath of the sage (as the poet puts it, though in the actual legend it was the sage's son) who cursed the garlander to die of a 'snakebite' within a week. The King's son, Prince Janmejaya, did all possible to avert the crisis. He performed a *yajna* for this. So powerful were the *mantras* of the pundits that snakes of all kinds came hurtling and fell headlong into his sacrifice, but one poisonous snake known as *takshak* remained stuck to the leg of Lord Indra's throne and somehow survived by changing its shape on the Lord's advice. That surviving snake ultimately bit the King who died resigned to his lot. After introducing this legend, the poet tells us about the killing of a poisonous scorpion by his uncle with the ivory dragonhead of his walking-stick in order to save his little son, Gopu. The legend is used here as an analogy to the latter incident.

The poems in which we have a direct mention of the Hindu gods and goddesses are: "Zoo Gardens Revisited", "The Difference" and "Moulting". In the first-named poem, Ramanujan invokes various Hindu gods to protect different kinds of animals to be found in the zoo— animals like flamingoes, monkeys, orangutans, giraffes, ostriches, tigers, tigresses, and chimps. The last lines of the poem must be quoted here:

Lord of lion face, boar snout, and fish eyes,
Killer of killer cranes, shepherd of rampant elephants,
Devour my lambs, devour them whole, save

them in the zoo garden ark of your belly.

(p. 47)

A number of incarnations of Lord Vishnu have been alluded to here. "Lord of lion face" is Narsingh (Half-Man and Half-Lion), who delivered the world from the clutches of Hiranya-Kashyapu, the tyrannical father of Prahlad, a great devotee of the Lord. "Boar snout" refers to the Lord's shape of Varaha, who lifted the stolen earth from the waters of the deep and thus freed it from the clutches of the demon-thief. Lord Vishnu also appeared as Matsya— "fish eyes" —in order to save Manu, the progenitor of the human race, from a great deluge. According to an Indian myth, the Lord rushed to the rescue of Gajendra from the jaws of a powerful crocodile. This myth is mentioned in the phrase "shepherd of rampant elephants". The Lord is also represented in our mythology as Kurma, the Tortoise, sitting on whose back he recovered some valuable things lost in the deluge. The Kurrna's back also served as the pivot of the mountain Mandara during the churning of the ocean in a tug-of-war between gods and demons. The Lord is also depicted as Kalki, the White Horse, who purged the creation. The expression "zoo garden ark of your belly" points to the Biblical story which tells us that the almighty God saved two of every kind of creature in Noah's ark when the entire creation was destined to meet deluge. In this way, Ramanujan has marvellously combined the Eastern and Western mythology in a harmonious whole, transcending thereby the local for the universal and the familiar for the mythical.

"The Difference" concentrates on the myth of Lord Vishnu assuming the shape of "the Dark One" —i.e. the God Vaman— who appeared before King Moradhvaj as a dwarf-beggar to test the latter's world-renowned generosity and charitable nature and who demanded of the King just three steps of earth. This is what Ramanujan gives us in this poem:

But today, out of the blue,
when Vishnu
came to mind, the Dark One you know
who began as a dwarf and rose in the
world to measure

heaven and earth with his paces ....

(p. 67-68)

With his three steps, the Lord measured "heaven and earth" as well as the underworld (which is not mentioned in the poem). Going a little beyond the text, we find that the testing of the King was still not over, for the lion on whom the Lord rode had eaten nothing so long and was terribly hungry. The King and his obedient spouse had nothing to feed the lion, as they were mere paupers presently. The Lord added to their woe and misery by pointing out that his chariot could eat nothing but the fresh flesh of their only son, and that too when the son is slashed into two halves by the royal couple without shedding even a drop of tear. The King now realised that it was a severe test for him. So, he and his wife took up the teethed saw in their hands and moved it over the head of their son, blinding their eyes. Instantly Lord Vishnu appeared in his true mettle and caught hold of the hands of the dumbfounded royal couple and pronounced glory and lasting fame for the King who had passed the heart-rending test with resounding success. The excellent poetic use to which Ramanujan has put this unforgettable Hindu myth of Lord Vishnu and King Moradhvaj speaks volumes of his grounding in the quintessence of Indian thought and tradition.

"Moulting" is a small prose poem, the last paragraph of which is pertinent enough from the viewpoint of Hindu religion and mythology. This paragraph runs as follows:

Lord of snakes and eagles, and everything in
Between, cover my son with an hour's shade and be
the thorn at a suitable height in this hour of change.

(p. 71)

The poet evidently invokes here the blessings of Garuda, the Lord of snakes and eagles, for the protection of his loved son, particularly at the hour of his physical change.

The fourth and final volume of Ramanujan poetry, *The Black Hen* (1995), contains three poems on Indian mythology. The first one deals with the Krishna-Pootna mythology in an unmistakable way. This is how the poet writes about it:

The breast she offered was full
of poison and milk.

Flashing eyes suddenly dull,
her voice was silk.

The child took her breast
in his mouth and sucked it right out of her chest.

Her carcass stretched from north to south.
She changed, undone by grace,
from deadly mother to happy demon,
found life in death[2].

This mythical tale relates to the dispatch of the she-demon, Pootna, by King Kansa to the abode of Yashoda, where *Krishna* was now being reared, with the sole objective of killing him. Pootna smeared her breasts of milk with poison, flew in a great hurry to Krishna's cradle and physically lifted him to let him suck her poisoned milk. The child Krishna sucked her breast, drew out her life-blood, and slew her instantly. At the time of her death, she appeared in her true shape to be redeemed by the Lord.

The second poem highlights the mythical tale of Hiranya-Kashyapu and Lord Vishnu. Ramanujan describes graphically "the perfect boon" demanded by the great demon-king:

When the clever man asks the perfect boon;
not to be slain by demon, god or by
beast, not by day nor by night,
by no manufactured weapon, not out
of doors nor inside, not in the sky
nor on earth,
    come now, come soon,
Vishnu, man, lion, neither and both, to hold
him in your lap to disembowel his pride
with the steel glint of bare claws at twilight.

(p. 226)

Hiranya-Kashyapu had pleased Brahma, the Creator of the Universe, with his severe penance and prayers. When Brahma appeared before him and asked him the desired boon, the demon-king demanded of him that he should not be slain by any demon, god or beast, neither by day nor by night, and that he should not fall a prey to "manufactured weapon", nor be killed out of doors nor inside, neither in the sky nor on earth. Very cleverly Brahma had granted this boon to him, though earlier he had turned down his demand of immortality. Ultimately, when Kashyapu's pitcher of sins was full to the brim and when his tortures of Prahlad had reached the highest scale, Lord Vishnu appeared in the shape of Narsingh, jumped ferociously upon Kashyapu, brought him down, rolled him in his lap, and slew him with his mighty "bare claws" at twilight.

The third mythological poem centers around a young female votary of Lord Shiva and her obduracy in refusing the advances of her new groom. She says to him:

> 'Keep off when I workship Shiva.
> Touch me three times, and you'll never
> see me again....'
>
> (p. 228)

Even when she lay in her bed, she used to intone 'Om, Om!' with every breath, but her man could think of nothing else but "her round breast,/ her musk, her darling navel and the rest." At last, his patience exhausted, and he touched her. At this, she "fled his hand as she would a spider" and "threw away her modesty." She now experienced a "new birth", the bliss of a married life. Here in this poem, Ramanujan has given a modernistic touch to the divine love; in fact, he has added a humanistic touch to an intense religious fervour (as that of the newly wedded woman).

From the foregoing observations, it is quite clear that the poet Ramanujan had a deep knowledge of Hindu religion and mythology, Hindu history and philosophy, and that he made a good creative use of it when he came to writing his own poetry. He is evidently fascinated with Hindu myths and legends and folk-tales, and uses them there where the necessity arises. For one thing, Ramanujan's love of Hindu religion and mythology (as witnessed in the last two volumes of his poetry) shows his bent of mind. Through it he unquestionably popularised Indian religion and culture in the West. For this reason, perhaps, he has been called "one of the most talented of the 'new' poets."[3]

As regards the marvellous treatment of Hindu mythology in his poetry, he resorts to it because it forms an integral part of the "cultural determinant"[4] of his fertile imagination.

REFERENCES

1. Ramanujan, A.K. *Second Sight* (Delhi: Oxford University Press, 1986), p. 16.

   -- Subsequent references to this text are absorbed in the paper itself.
2. Ramanujan, A. K. *The Black Hen* (Delhi: Oxford University Press, 1995), p. 221.

   -- Subsequent references to this text are given in the paper itself.
3. Iyengar, K. R. Srinivas. *Indian Writing in English,* 4th ed. (New Delhi: Sterling Publishers Pvt. Ltd., 1984), p. 671.
4. Kulshrestha, Chirantan, "The Self in Ramanujan's Poetry", *The Indian Journal of English Studies*", XVIII (1978-79), p. 110.

Fiction

Identity as Ideological Strategy: Reading Hari Kunzru's *The Impressionist*

4

Banibrata Mahanta

The Impressionist, the eponymous hero as well as the novel is born out of the author Hari Kunzru's need to articulate and examine his origin and place in the world. This paper attempts to examine the linkages between identity, locatedness and canon by mapping the repeated transformations of the protagonist of the novel with respect to the coordinates of gender, race, class and sexuality. The paper is divided into two parts. The first part attempts to read Kunzru's novel as an examination, challenge and subversion of the essentialist position on identity. In the second part, the issue of how identity formation was used as a strategic ideological weapon propped up by the British literary canon is examined. Certain British texts used by Kunzru in *The Impressionist* with a view to subverting the ideology of the canon are also discussed.

I

The concept of identity is at the core of all theoretical debates, be it in psychoanalysis, poststructuralism or cultural studies. All the existing debate about the concept of identity, ranging from the late nineteenth century to now only serves to bring to the fore the ontological, epistemological and political limitations of the term.

Hari Kunzru's first novel, *The Impressionist*, thematises the idea that identity as a concept cannot be basic, invariable or pre-social in nature. Pran Nath, the illegitimate child of Amrita and British arborist Ronald Forrester, is born after Amrita's marriage to Pandit Amar Nath Razdan of Agra, who is a distinguished court pleader. By virtue of his birth, Pran Nath becomes the legal heir to Pandit Razdan's fortune. When Pran

Nath is fifteen years old, Pandit Razdan succumbs to an influenza epidemic which strikes Agra. However, before his death, he learns of Pran Nath's true parentage and throws the boy out of his house. Thus, begins the process of self-discovery for Pran Nath— "the near mythical journey of a young man who must invent himself to survive— not once but many times — the impressionist" (Reading Group Guides).

From India to Britain to Africa, and from Rukhsana to Pretty Bobby to Jonathan Bridgeman, the Impressionist moves from place to place and from identity to identity. In Pran Nath's travels from one identity to another, what is examined is not simply the construction of his identity, but the discursive and disciplinary places from where questions of identity are strategically and institutionally posed. The fact that Pran Nath's identity is problematic and fluid, and also circumstantial, is emphasised by the reading of his horoscope at birth:

> The astrologer could predict none of the usual things... Patterns emerged, only to fade when another aspect of the conjunction was considered. Planets seemed to flit through houses, hovering between benign and malevolent positions. Clusters of possibilities formed... .(26)

The idea of 'home', of 'identity' is what is examined in the first episode in Pran's life. One's 'home', ties and relations are determined and circumscribed by the possibilities of circumstance. Pran's initial lie, till he is discovered to be an illegitimate half-caste, is thus as spoilt child-heir in a Kashmiri-Brahmin household. No one in the household likes him, but they tolerate his brattishness because of his 'identity'. Ironically, once disgraced, the same people look on him differently. That Pandit Amar Nath Razdan is for sometime Pran Nath's father is ironic because Pandit Razdan's views about the world are informed by his caste. He is "sternly disapproving of all relaxations of caste restriction", "a staunch advocate of rigorous personal hygiene", and even with regard to language, "a fierce opponent of debased or impure usage, impropriety, profanity and slang" (30). In short, he is terrified of any sort of pollution, maintaining "impermeable boundaries between himself and the world's filth" (31). His unquestioning acceptance of Pran as his own blood, and his boasting about Pran's complexion and features as being the result his own ancestry (till his actual origins are not known) are ironical, and indicative of the line Kunzru is to take in the novel.

Once, he is thrown out of Pandit Razdan's house, Pran Nath is advised by a beggar who sits in front of his house to go and meet the Anglo-Indian community, the 'blackie-whites'. The picture of the lives of the Anglo-Indian community that Kunzru portrays is full of pathos, and bitterly ironical. They do not associate with the country of their birth, living their lives in ironic mimicry of the British, calling England their "home", yearning to be "as white as a tennis shoe" (49).

If caste and nationality as identity-markers are challenged in the Razdan home, Pran Nath's encounter with the Anglo-Indian community foregrounds the issue of kinship and blood. Till the secret of his birth becomes common knowledge, Pran Nath passes off as a Kashmiri Brahmin. And though he is the same blood as the Anglo-Indian community, he is not accepted by them. And later in the novel, he passes off as an Englishman. Homeless and rootless, he is unable to define himself:

> [H]e tries to parse the problem. You are what you feel. Or if not you should feel like what you are. But if you are something you don't know yourself to be, what are the signs? What is the feeling of not being who you think you are? (52)

Driven away from the Razdan house and rejected by the Anglo-Indian community, the protagonist finds shelter in a whorehouse, from where he is dressed up as a girl, Rukhsana, and sold to the Nawab of Fatehpur, to be used as bait for the paedophilic British officer, Major Privett-Clampe. This episode in the protagonist's life, where he is transformed from boy to girl and then almost castrated, and then used to bait the Major, questions gender and sexuality as sources of identity bringing in the issue of body politics. If Pran Nath can simultaneously pass off as a boy, a girl/eunuch and a bait for a gay major, what is he really?

Here, the protagonist is contrasted with the childless Nawab of Fatehpur, whose impotency is linked to his identity as the king who cannot produce a heir; secondly, he is contrasted with the Nawab's sexually degenerate younger brother Firoze and his Bohemian ways; then, the eunuchs who look after the Nawab of Fatehpur's harem; lastly, Pran is contrasted with the paedophilic major.

Besides interrogating gender and sexuality as sites for constructing identity, these parallels are also used to comment tellingly on the institutions of the Raj, their machinations and pettiness. Major Privett-Clampe is a study in the degradation and arbitrariness of the empire. His predicaments as well as his predilections are in stark contrast to all the high sounding rhetoric about 'civilising missions' meant for 'inferior races'. Sir Wyndham Braddock, the officer visiting Fatehpur, is also commented on in a similar vein, as is the kleptomaniac Lady Braddock and the 'military' Augusta Privett-Clampe.

Privett-Clampe, however, suffers an attack of conscience after attempting to sodomise Pran Nath and decides, in repentance, to educate him and to make an Englishman out of him. He is named Clive, dressed up as an English schoolboy, and taught English Literature, which includes Kipling.

It is in the next section, where the protagonist lives his double life as Robert/Chandra and Pretty Bobby, that we get a detailed understanding of his character. That he is a creature of the surface who refuses to look inwards is understandable, because his past experiences do not bear much looking into. This makes him want to live an "unexamined life", not going into the heart of things: "Bobby is a creature of surface.... Bobby's skin is not a boundary between things but the thing itself, a screen on which certain effects take place" (250). Even his guardians, the Rev Andrew Macfarlane and his wife Elspeth feel his "chameleon" like qualities, his ability to 'absorb' things and become 'part' of his surroundings:

> Bobby has a quality which is different from secretiveness. When he is talking to you, he seems to fall in which the rhythm of your voice. He will stand how you stand, making remarks that seem tailormade to your sense of humour. For all his swagger and beauty and flamboyance, there is something in Bobby which craves invisibility. (237)

In the Bombay episode, Kunzru compares ideology and identity. The Rev. Macfarlane's degeneration from an idealistic young colonial missionary to the horror he has become in middle-age doesn't affect his identity. He has gone from missionary to skull collector to craniologist, but he is still the Rev. Macfarlane. And his obsession with craniology harks back to the idea of racism as the basis for superiority, telling us that Rev. Macfarlane is unchallenged in his position (even though he has changed) just because he happens to be white skinned. Against a stated ideology and scheme, Macfarlane's activities appear immoral and reprehensible. The protagonist's activities on the other hand, equally immoral in the same scheme of things, leave one curiously without any feeling. One feels that given his circumstances, he had no option but to behave as he does. Thus morality, values and scales of judgement, which also go into the constituting of identity, are shown by Kunzru to be relative.

In the last part of the novel, the Impressionist takes up the identity of Jonathan Bridgeman, an English student who is killed in anti-colonial riots in Mumbai. The protagonist takes his place aboard the ship that sails to England and settles down to life there as Jonathan. How easily he makes his way into white/British institutions again highlights the shaky foundations of the intellectual, social, moral and political structures of imperialism. In the school in which the Impressionist passes off as Bridgeman, there is an orchidist headmaster, another flagbearer of imperialism, who lectures him, ironically, against hybridity:

> Surely, as observers of creation, we must look upon these boundaries as a good thing. Were there none, the flowers would lose their identities in a hybrid swarm and nature would be in a desperate mess. (310)

That a representative of the 'mess' he is talking about is standing in front of him, unrecognised, tells its own story, as does the fact that the Impressionist is rejected as a lover by Astarte Chapel for being too English, "too conventional" (415).

Identity comes from believing, and the Impressionist does not believe in anything. He simply is. And "his life has taught him one thing...belief is optional" (356). 'Pran'— the name is significant in his context. Pran means spirit and life in its essence and spirit and life cannot be categorised by race, gender, sex or nationality.

If imperialism was built on an idea, the corrosion of that idea is what Kunzru focuses on in the protagonist's journey to Africa. How the Fotse tribe of Africa is trampled over in course of the onward march of imperialism inverts the very logic of all pretensions of 'progress' that imperialism purports to bring. Identity vis-a-vis imperialism is thus nothing but adherence to a set of beliefs. As the eunuch tells Rukhsana: "You may think you are singular. You may think you are incapable of change. But we are all as unstable as the air" (82). So, the protagonist's Britishness too finally gives way to his journey towards another identity. And this is the note on which the novel ends:

> The journey is everything. He has no thoughts of arriving anywhere. Tonight he will sleep under the enormous bowl of the sky. Tomorrow he will travel on. (481)

II

Language and literature are inextricably linked with notions of citizenship, society and the ways we get along with others in the world. Kunzru, in an interview to bookclub.co.nz, admits to being intrigued by the fact that literary ideas of Indian and the colony were constructed through 'English' literature:

> What most of those books seem to me to do, is present a British subject who is placed in this alien context with all this overloaded sensory excitement, which is all challenging the bounds of proportion, decency and correctness that constitute proper Britishness. English Literature with a capital E and a capital L is all about teaching the reader how to be British in the colonies. Showing what it means to be really English.

Identity as concept and identity-politics as practice is the intertextual strategy that Kunzru employs to question this political enterprise of English Literature which evolved as a discipline in the nineteenth century because (in the Indian context) of the British East India Company's desire to teach the native population how to become good company servants:

> The literature of England was seen as a mould of the English way of life, morals, taste and the English way of doing things; why not teach Indians how to be more English by teaching them English Literature? Studying English Literature was seen as a way of 'civilizing' the native population. (Eaglestone 11)

Kunzru's book deals with narrative representation of identity and its politics in four identifiable novels—*A Passage to India, Maurice, Kim and Heart of Darkness*—and how these exemplify a certain ideology.

E.M. Forster's *A Passage to India* does not put forth any solution to what really happened in the Marabar caves. If anything, there is an attempt to mythify the incident in a way that serves to reinforce the superiority of the British. The echoes of Adela Quested's shriek, which reverberated through the Marabar caves and throughout *A Passage to India* are laid to rest in the cave scene at the beginning of Kunzru's novel. If Adela and Dr. Aziz had consummated their relationship, the Impressionist is what might have been the result. Kunzru leaves Amrita and Ronald Forrester in the cave, stripped of all identity except the primal one. The illegitimate child born out of this union serves to subvert Forster's idea of the superior race building a bridge to reach out to the inferior one. If anything, the Impressionist's adventures only serve the show how shaky and questionable the concepts of Englishness and imperialism are.

Pran Nath uses all his powers of deception and trickery to go to England where he is unquestioningly accepted as an Englishman. In fact, he is so successful in impersonating and living life as Jonathan Bridgeman, a typical English youth, that he is rejected by the girl he is courting for being too British and too boring:

> You're the most conventional person I know....You like following the rules, having everything just so. I want to get away from it, it's stifling doing what you were born to do... . (415)

What this serves to underline is that identity is not something you are born with, but something that is acquired in response to surroundings. What Rushdie said in a different context is equally applicable here: the form of the pickle jar shapes the contents that are in it, the shape of the jar is incidental (459).

Clive, the name that Privett-Clampe gives the Impressionist when he decides to educate him, harks back to the character of Clive in E.M. Forster's *Maurice*. Clive, in the latter work, views his homosexuality as a Platonic feeling, filling the carnal/erotic space in his relationship with Maurice with arid academic theorising. And later, in order to take his place in regular British society—in the family, the countryside, the parish and in politics—Clive conveniently suppresses his personal predelictions to go along with society, to conform.

Rudyard Kipling's *Kim* is another novel that Kunzru refers to repeatedly in *The Impressionist* as well as in his interviews. The epigraph of the novel is also from *Kim*. Classifying his hero as picaresque, Kunzru says in an interview to Frederick Luis Aldama:

> The central character is very much this type of hero—an outsider—with a skewed pair of eyes looking on a crazy world.

There are parallels not just between the characters of Kim and the Impressionist, but also between Kipling and Kunzru. The character of Kim, a white Irish boy who has grown up on the streets of Lahore as an orphan, "a poor white of the very poorest", links him to the 'urchin' Pran Nath *(Kim 49)*. However, unlike Pran Nath, Kim occupies a privileged position by virtue of his being a member of the white, English, ruling class. This position of prominence is reinforced by the textual subjugation of Babu Hurree Chander Mookerjee inspite of the fact that he is well educated and has a determined place in society. In privileging Kim, Kipling stresses the superiority of the 'white man' and male domination in the wider context of colonial repression. Thus, the racist and sexist position of *Kim is* what Kunzru provides a counter-narrative to in his novel.

The last part of *The Impressionist*, which deals with the adventures of Jonathan Bridgeman in Africa, writes back to British canonical readings of Joseph Conrad's *Heart of Darkness*. Kunzru tells Aldama:

> As you probably realized throughout the book, there's a lot of fooling around with English literature dealing with India—and colonial literature more generally. In the latter stages of the novel, they go up a river in Africa, but instead of Conrad's river in *Heart of Darkness* that's all about varticality and closing in as they move more and more to the center. In Jonathan's case the story opens out into this terrible blankness. So, I play a lot of games with the colonial literary canon.

That Kunzru has Conrad's novel in mind while writing the last part of his novel is also clear from the fact that the ship which takes Bridgeman to Africa is the *Nelly*, while the ship aboard which Marlow narrates his tale is called the *Nellie*.

Forster's mythification of the East-West encounter, Kipling's furthering of the same and Conrad's situating of the colony as a site for activity are all turned inside out. The myth of the Adela-Aziz encounter is set against the real encounter between Amrita and Ronald Forrester, Pran Nath offsets Kim, while Bridgeman is posited in contrast with Marlow.

In *Heart of Darkness,* Marlow talks of reaching a particular destination and of the fact that the 'idea' behind anything is important:

> The conquest of the earth, which mostly means the taking it away from those who have a different complexion or slightly flatter noses than ourselves, is not a pretty thing when you look into it too much. What redeems it is the idea only. An idea at the back of it; not a sentimental pretence but an idea; and an unselfish belief in the idea—something you can set up, and bow down before, and offer a sacrifice to. (141)

This 'idea' that constructs the identity of the coloniser and his 'civilising mission', may, on the face of it, have echoes of a religion, cult or faith, but is actually quite absurd when examined from a different perspective:

> I find it quite hard not to be moved by the idea of some 20-year old boy coming out and more or less being put in a tent in some thousands and thousands of square miles of territory and being told "rule it!" The ideological strategy

> and the sense of belief that they must have had...this absurd self-belief—you know, a lone figure a thousand miles away from anybody and he will still dress for dinner! I suppose in some ways the book is about...how Britishness was elevated to this quasi-religious rationale for extraordinary things. (bookclub.co.nz)

Lennard Davis describes the interrelation between literature and ideology as follows: Novels do not depict life, they depict life as it is represented by ideology. Ideology, that is how a culture represents itself, makes narrative representations appear normal by making it appear natural or common-sensical (24-25): the meaning constructed is made to appear like something *inherent* in that which is being represented. Kunzru attempts, through his novel, to repudiate and parody this representation.

Susannah Meadows, reviewing *The Impressionist,* criticises Kunzru for creating a hero who is too flimsy:

> With such a flimsy protagonist, the centre has no chance of holding... Pran Nath is indeed a completely blank, stunted paper doll of a character. That's the problem. There is so little development that each incarnation of Pran Nath is like a new outfit tabbed onto his paper-thin personality, with no accessory left over from the former life on which to build the new.

Kunzru counters this criticism by saying that this is precisely the impression that he wants to give. The novel is constructed to disorient its readers on the level of narration. This is what he has to tell Aldama:

> Like the heroes of picaresque novels, he is something of a blank slate; he lacks an identity. So, the colour of the book does not come out of any psychological depth of his character, but rather as he moves from set-piece scene to set-piece scene as the pageantry of the Empire plays out all around.

The way in which the novel interrogates identity from every possible perspective marks Kunzru's vision as fundamentally reactionary. He is attempting to see through a convenient stratification of reality. Considering that Kunzru is of mixed parentage, there is a correspondence between his protagonist and himself, both trying to figure out their respective positions in the world:

> I remember, as a kid, sitting with luggage on platform stations in India, attracting a crowd of a hundred, two hundred people! They would sit and just watch. Very, very weird. When you are a little kid, you are quite conservative about what's normal and what's not normal and I was used to my normal world of suburban London (BBC Books).

Living in Britain, travelling to India, relating to the former, but unable to negate the latter, the author was caught in a double-bind that did not let him be comfortable with totalising positions or unambiguous paradigms, actual or conceptual. He feels strongly about his experiences as well as the experience of other mixed race people and immigrants. Further, Kunzru also feels strongly about mythifying of identity—identity is not a given thing. This is what drives him to question and subvert identity and foreground its ambivalence. He tells Aldama:

> In *The Impressionist* I decided that this was a very personal project. It was a project that I needed to undertake in order to examine certain things about where I came from and what I felt my position in the world was.

The fact that the novel does not end in the conventional way is perhaps indicative of Kunzru's acceptance of his protagonist's and his own fluid position without granting any concessions or making any compromises.

REFERENCES

Kunzru, Hari. *The Impressionist*. New Delhi: Penguin, 2003. (all quotations from the text are from this edition of book).

Kunzru, Hari. "Conversations". 2001. 1 January, 2002. http://www.bookclub.co.nz/ features/harikunzru.htm.

Eaglestone, R. *Doing English*. London and New York: Routledge, 2000.

Davis, Lennard J. *Resisting Novels: Ideology and Fiction*. New York and London: Methuen, 1987.

Rushdie, Salman. *Midnight's Children*. London. Picador, 1981.

Forster, E.M. *A Passage to India*. 1924. Harmondsworth: Penguin, 1979.

Forster, E.M. *Maurice.* Vikas: Delhi, 1971.

Kipling, Rudyard. *Kim.* London: Wordsworth, 1993.

Kunzru, Hari. Interview with Frederick Luis Aldama. 11 Oct. 2004, 23 Dec. 2005 http://www.humanitiesretooled.org/index.php?sm=hrt_editorial.php&modCMC_cidd = 175&PHP/

Conrad, Joseph. *Heart of Darkness.* 1902. *Heart of Darkness and Other Tales*. Ed. Cedric Watts, Oxford: OUP, 1990.

Meadows, Susannah. "Son of a Sort of Goddess". Rev. of *The Impressionist,* by Hari Kunzru. *New York Times* on the Web. 12 May, 2002. http://www.nytimes/com.

"Hari Kunzru". *BBC Books.* 2 March 2004. http://www.bbc.co.uk/arts/books/author/kunzru/index.shtml.

Scapegoating as a Motif in Morrison's *The Bluest Eye*

5

R.P. Pradhan

More than any other feature the motif of scapegoating seems to dominate *The Bluest Eye* of Toni Morrison. As an African-American novelist, she writes in Black literary tradition with a feminist outlook. She refers to the disparity between the worlds of Whites and Blacks and portrays how Pecola's overvaluation of White beauty causes in her a feeling of self-hatred and brings about her tragedy. Pecola wants blue eyes that symbolise white beauty and that will make her lovely and attractive. As her dreams and aspirations are shadowy and inaccessible, they make her undergo a state of sufferings and spiritual tortures.

Pecola Breedlove, the central character of the novel is made to bear the blame that should be shifted to other and thus, becomes a scapegoat. The whole society of Blacks and Whites is hostile to her and victimises her. She is crushed under the machinery of race and gender. The poor Black girl is caught in an illusion of the western notion of physical beauty—white skin with blue eyes and blond hair. The idea is essentially racist. The novelist explores the disastrous consequences of such notions of beauty. It equates white skin not only with personal virtues and worth but also with political powers that dominate a nation and give global publicity. Such conception implies that those who do not possess such features are ugly and inferior. Such idea damages one's self-image and destroys happiness.

The tragedy of Pecola is in part born out of her own character and in part it is also the product of the racist and gender factors of the American society. The scale is heavier on the side of the victimising which is inflicted by the society. No doubt, Pecola herself is attracted by the Pop-culture of America which is reinforced by popular cinema and other media which glamorise white standard and values of beauty but there is no denying the fact that the external circumstances caused by the instinct of colour and gender contribute to the total annihilation of her personality. Pecola becomes more and more conscious of her deformity. The poor and loveless condition of her Black family also adds to her further degradation in this matter.

The family of Breed loves is at the very bottom of the hierarchy. At the top are the whites and just below the whites are the light complexioned Blacks. In the third order there come the sugar brown migrants from other places and the niggers are at the lowest. The white people carry the ancestral idea that all civilisations are derived from the white race, that a society is great and brilliant in so for as it preserves the blood of the white race. Pecola beomes the victim of such conception. She accepts the conventional standard of white beauty and aspires for having blue eyes. She regards the blue eyes the miraculous beauty which may be bestowed on her by the church. She offers prayer for that. Her fanciful quest for blue eyes is bound to end in failure and it drives her on the brink of insanity.

Pecola's obsession with the myth of physical beauty makes her life devoid of joy. She loses her sense of self-identity and is subjected to humiliation and mental depression. She is told from the day of her birth that she is ugly. The surname of Breedlove in ironical manner does not breed love, it only breeds a feeling of self-hatred and mutual destruction. The members of the family all believe themselves that they are ugly and ugliness becomes an all pervading feature in their home:

> It was as though some mysterious all-knowing master had said, " you are ugly people." They had looked about themselves and saw nothing to contradict the statement; saw, in fact, support for it leaping at them from every billboard, every movie, every glance...........And they took the ugliness in their hands, threw it as a mantle over them, and went about the world with it.[1]

Throughout the novel Pecola is used as the sacrificial victim. She is a completely defenceless creature who cannot fight back the harm done to her. The novel concentrates on her victimisation by her own people. They have not learnt to accept their blackness. The black pursuit of the white standard of beauty runs throughout the novel.

The final act of victimisation in the novel occurs at the moment when Pecola's father himself rapes her. He ought to have shielded her from harm but he does just the reverse. Pecola's has been pregnant by her father. Her entire community wants that Pecola's baby should die and the baby dies. No sympathy has been expressed for suffering Pecola. The event is not taken to be so awful and horrifying as it is supposed to be in other cases. The novelist refers to the sad event in this way:

> I tell you at the beginning of *The Bluest Eye* on the very first page what happened, but now I want you to go with me and look at this, so when you get to the scene where the father rapes the daughter, which is as awful a thing, I suppose, as can be imagined, by the time you get there it's almost irrelevant because I want you to look at him and his love for his daughter and his powerlessness to help her pain. By that time his embrace, the rape, is all the gift he has left.[2]

Morrison wants us to understand the circumstances of rape and Cholly's state of mind which led to the fatal rape of his daughter. It has been pointed out that Cholly wants to show love and give something of himself to her but he is incapable of doing that. The only thing he thinks he can offer to her is his manhood. In that condition, his rape is an expression of his love that appears to be violent. As Nellie Mckay suggests:

> Within the novel Morrison demonstrates that even with the best intentions, people hurt each other when they are chained to circumstances of poverty and low social status. 'Violence' says Morrison, is a distortion of what, perhaps, we want to do."[3]

It is for this reason that the novelist calls Cholly's life tragic.

Claudia, the young black girl who has been a schoolmate of Pecola and who is also the narrator of the event of the novel acknowledges at the end:

> Cholly loved her. I'm sure he did. He, at any rate, was the one who loved her enough to touch her, envelope her, give something of himself to her. But his touch was fatal, and the something he gave her filled the matrix of her agony with death. Love is never any better than the lover.[4]

The novelist enables us to peep into the affairs of love among the blacks who are living in the racist society of America. In that condition, their love is distorted. Pecola's father Cholly is a drunkard. He always quarrels with his wife Pauline in a violent manner. He becomes a frustrated man and loses all ambitions and hopes of life. He has failed as a husband and he also fails as a father. When he comes home on the day of the fatal event of rape he is quite drunk. His emotions at that time are confused. He has got a sense of guilt that he is helpless to do anything for his daughter. It is in this state of mind that he comes close to his daughter for the forbidden act. In this way, Cholly's action has been given some sort of excuse.

In the context of Pecola, Morrison is critical of Black women who run after the idea of white beauty and poison the atmosphere of the Black community. She refers to certain rituals that are prevalent in the Black society. They are related to some magical performance which is supposed to give power to the doer. Magic implies the seeking of power by the powerless people and the black are powerless. Henry Washington makes use of magic to attract the love of Claudia and Frieda. Claudia and Frieda also take resort to magic in order to help Pecola and her unborn child. Pecola also seeks magic or miracle which might make her free from her poor and ugly existence. She goes to Soaphead, the interpreter of 'Dreams' to make a request that he should give her blue eyes. In the beginning, he tells her that he is not a magician or worker of miracle to help her in that matter but Claudia persists in achieving her ideals and makes him ready to do that. Soaphead follows a ritual to give her a belief that the impossible has happened. In this way, Pecola finds consolation in miracles and magic.

The power of magic may be seen in the general conversation in which Pecola is blamed for her rape and the unborn child is wished to be dead. Claudia and Frieda want to save Pecola and her child and follow the course of magic. They regard magic as a healing force. In their opinion, magic is related to life and nature. It is also connected with their love and compassion for Pecola. In this way, they plant seeds and sing magical songs over them so that they might grow. They have got a firm belief that just as the seeds should sprout and grow, the baby of Pecola would also grow. The seeds of Claudia and Frieda never grow, it is because the soil is barren and magic cannot make it fertile. This ritual of growing seeds ends in failure.

Pecola also performs some different types of rituals. She gives poisoned meat to an old dog and perceives his reactions to being a sign that blue eyes will be bestowed upon her. This sign which is given to Pecola is not natural. It is contrived by Soaphead and it is not magical but in the mind of Pecola it gains ground and takes effect. These rituals disappoint Pecola, her child dies and Pecola goes insane. There is no recourse left for her but to go into madness. She flutters round aimlessly like a bird trying to fly away into the endless sky but it cannot because it is crippled:

> The birdlike gestures are worn away to a mere picking and plucking her way between the tire rims and the sunflowers, between coke bottles and milkweed, among all the waste and beauty of the world which is what she herself was.[5]

Pecola cannot fly away in the sky. She remains tied to the ground. Her situation is a reminder to the community of its collective guilt which is imposed upon Pecola. The community cannot improve itself. Its contempt for Pecola goes on increasing. She may stay in the community but really she is relegated to a spot among the insane persons. Like them, she is tolerated but she is ignored all the time as harmless creature. The scapegoat is thrown into infertile soil to die because it has got no chance to remain alive.

Cholly, the husband, Pauline, the wife, Sammy, the son and Pecola, the daughter constitute the poor black Breedloves family. The family perceives itself to be ugly in contrast to the white standard of beauty. It is passing a loveless quarrelsome life. Pecola finds herself lonely and despised at school. Claudia and Frieda rescue her one afternoon from the black boys while she is walking back from school. The boys are tormenting her with racial and sexual abuses. The winter section describes the black women who have migrated from the South Africa and have adopted the culture of white values. One of them is Geraldine who regards herself neat and "quiet" and hates the niggers who are in her opinion " dirty and loud." Her son Junior lures Pecola into his house and flings his cat at her in a cruel manner and then blames her for killing it. As a result of that, Pecola is pushed out by his mother as a "nasty little black bitch."[6]

The Bluest Eye, the first novel of Toni Morrison is also a quest novel. It is dominated by women characters. Its major aim seems to be the portrayal of a black woman who wants to thrive in life and ride on a high ladder in the face of white domination. The novelist refers to an excerpt from a white school Primer which is extensively taught in all the schools of White and Black in United States. It describes the white ideal of a happy home and family with father, mother, brother, daughter, friend—their mutual love and their love for the cat and the dog. This ideal is represented by the Fisher family in the novel. Pecola's mother works in this family. Pauline finds that this white family is not happy in spite of the possessions of money and comforts. She finds it sloppy and dirty. The white woman interferes with Pauline's work as if she knows more about cleanliness. The white woman further asks her to make a choice between herself and her husband Cholly: "She said she would let me stay if I left him. I thought about that. But later on, it didn't seem none too bright for a Black woman to leave a Black man for a white woman."[7] The white woman feels insulted when Pauline chooses to stay with her man. It shows the attitude of white man's society towards the Black, how a Black woman is crushed. The story, thus, is viewed and told from female perspective. The narrator who is a young black girl is observer and participant in the story. She faces the same challenge posed by the destructive myth of white beauty which pervades the black community.

Pecola's story moves from pathos to tragedy and finally to a state of madness. Claudia, the narrator does not present a systematic account of Pecolas life rather she states the key-episodes of her life. The style of her narration becomes elliptical. The presentation of the story is symbolical. It is divided into the seasons of autumn, winter, spring and summer. The gap in the story is filled up by the omniscient narrator. In the section of autumn, Claudia recalls her own family and describes Pecola's brief stay in her house. The omniscient narrator further describes the plight of the house of Breedloves and also how the members of the family lead a sad and unhappy life which is full of violence. In the winter section, Claudia narrates how Pecola is tormented by the Black boys and how she is saved by Claudia and her sister Frieda. There is further description that at home, their roomer is entertaining two prostitutes. In the section of the spring, Claudia makes report that her parents throw their roomer Henry out because he had been trying to molest Frieda. The section further describes how Pauline as a young woman is addicted to witnessing movies from where she has derived all her values of life. They are all white values which are related to her dreams of beauty and love. In course of time, her dreams of happy life are shattered because when Pecola is born, she knows that Pecola is ugly. Finally, the mother becomes an ideal servant in a white family. In the section of summer, Claudia recalls the story of Pecola's rape by her father and the vain attempt of Claudia and her sister to make Pecola's baby alive. Further, Claudia sums up Pecola's sad story and tells us how Claudia accepts her share of blame for making the unfortunate girl Pecola, a pariah and scapegoat.

Pecola thinks that her possession of blue eyes would be a remedy for all types of diseases. In that way she would be able to reduce the violent quarrels between her father and mother. She would also be elevated above her black community. The nature of her prayer for blue eyes has been expressed by the novelist in this way:

> Pretty eyes. Pretty blue eyes. Big blue pretty eyes. Run, Jip, run. Jip runs, Alice runs. Alice has blue eyes. Jerry has blue eyes. Jerry runs. Alice runs. They run with their blue eyes. Four blue eyes. Four pretty blue eyes. Blue-sky eyes. Blue-like Mrs. Forrest's blue blouse eyes. Morning-glory-blue eyes. Alice-and-Jerry-blue-storybook-eyes.[8]

The tragedy of Pecola may be attributed to the problem of colour. It has been pointed out that the Black people in U.S. start with the assumption that Black is evil, Black is sinful, Black is devil. The evil and ugliness of blackness has been contrasted in the popular mind with the goodness and purity of whiteness. The domination of the whites over the Blacks in the U.S.A. is born out of the idea that the Black race by nature is incapable of enjoying freedom and it is marked out only for slavery. This pernicious and destructive belief found a way into a theory. A French diplomat and ethnologist, Count Joseph Arthur De Gobineau, who is called the father of racism, erected this pernicious belief into a theory: "I..... have no hesitation in regarding the white face as superior to all others in beauty...... Human groups are unequal in beauty; and this inequality is rational, logical, permanent, and indestructible."[9]

The idea of the inherent superiority of the white over the Black is pervading to this day in the U.S.A. In America, black skin is associated with thick lips and kinky hair whereas the white colour is associated with straight hair, blue eyes and good looks. The traditional white notion of beauty is reaffirmed by Knight Dunlap, a Professor at the prestigious John Hopkins University at Baltimore:

> The type which is highest in value tends to approximate the European type, wherever the European type becomes known. All dark races prefer white skin...
>
> The broad flat nose and thick wide lips are often repulsive because they suggest the African, if for no other reason. But I suspect that the thick lips are also a defect because they are in themselves a hindrance to efficient speech.[10]

Such white notion of beauty has sunk deep into the mind of the African Americans. It results in the act of self-loathing, psychological operation and loss of identity. These standards of white beauty damage the black women more than black men. Pecola becomes a natural scapegoat in such situation. This complex idea of colour is at the bottom of the tragedy of Pecola. The beauty culture in American society tells upon her life.

The novel ends on a note of tragedy. Pecola is deceived into believing that she has acquired blue eyes and in this way loses her sanity of mind. She is treated as a pariah living on the periphery of the village in the company of her mother. However, the novel does not end without hope. Claudia and Frieda do not surrender to the myth of white beauty. Community or the neighbourhood is a very strong factor in the novels of Toni Morrison. In *The Bluest Eye* the community gives life and sustenance to the people. Pecola is victim of illusory ideals but these two sisters are very much realistic in their outlook. The novel is not merely the story of Pecola but it deals with the entire Black Community. It is not depressive because the fighting instincts of other characters like Claudia are there. However, a single character like Pecola is isolated and segregated from society and is made the scapegoat.

REFERENCES

1. Toni Morrison. *The Bluest Eye* (New York: Pocket Books, 1970), p. 34.
2. Barbara Hill Rigney. *The Voices of Toni Morrison* (Columbus: Ohio State University Press, 1991), 32, quoted in *Literature and its times*, vol. 4-53.
3. Nellie McKay. "An Interview with Toni Morrison" in *Toni Morrison; Critical Perspective*, 397.
4. Toni Morrison. *The Bluest Eye* (New York: Pocket Books, 1970), p. 96.
5. *Ibid.*, 159.
6. *Ibid.*, 102.
7. *Ibid.*, 95.
8. *Ibid.*, 176.
9. Quoted in Donald B. Gibson. "Text and Countertext in *The Bluest Eye*" in *Toni Morrison: Critical Perspectives Past and Present,* eds. Henry Louis Gates Jr.et.al., 159.
10. "Personal Beauty and Racial Betterment" (St. Louis: C.V. Mosby, 1920), 32, quoted in '*The Bluest Eye* by Toni Morrison', *Literature and its Times*, Vol. 4, Joyce Moss and George Wilson (Detroit: Gale, 1997), 49.

East-West Confrontation in Markandaya's *The Nowhere Man* (1972)

6

A.N. Dwivedi and O.P. Dwivedi

East is East, West is West,
and ne'er the twain shall meet.
— Rudyard Kipling

In this postcolonial era, an unprecedented predicament resulting in confusion and conflict has plagued the masses across the globe and Kamala Markandaya is no exception to this. Markandaya, a pioneer of the Indian diaspora, put the Indian English literature on a global map. Her novels forcefully portray the people of the East and the West and the inevitable confrontation between them on issues of races, cultures and modes of living. Her mixed sensibility allows her to properly balance the Oriental and Occidental values of life. Dorien Macdermott rightly points out:

> Markandaya has acquired a duality of vision, enabling her to observe both British and Indians with cool detachment... as she herself has said, in spite of being an outsider by choice, 'the eyes I see with are still Indian eyes.'[1]

And Balachandra Rajan also comments about her mixed sensibility— that "the presence of two cultures in one's mind forms a wider and therefore a saner basis on which to originate the quest for identity and that the disordance between these cultures can be creative as well as merely confusing",[2] but his phrase 'confusing' could not pervade Markandaya's imaginative fictional world. Here in this paper, we propose to deal with the East-West confrontation, arising from social and cultural considerations, in Markandaya's novel, *The Nowhere Man* (1972).

The Nowhere Man brings to the fore the problem of transculturation and the relationship of the Orients and the Occidents. The novel revolves round the central figure of

Srinivas, who is suffering from a sense of alienation in life. Srinivas is a victim of British barbarism in India before he leaves for England along with his wife Vasantha. Srinivas starts an import-export business of spices in England, and is blessed with two sons—Sheshu and Laxman. The identity problems besiege the two children as they advance in age. They have acquired the western ways of size and the disclosure of Laxman to marry an English girl Pat came as a shock to Srinivas and his wife. Immediately, Sheshu succumbs to his injuries in a war, fighting for England. Srinivas's colonial hangover gets a fresh jolt. Markandaya foreshadows many diasporic concerns and she clears the presuppositions of the third-world people who are quite keen on entering into the first world, with aspirations for better wealth and prosperity, without realising that the displacement to the first world demands greater adaptability, both in terms of culture and climate. There is a big vacuum between these two worlds which is very difficult to fill up. Markandaya warns the Indians by revealing to them poignancy of demonic humanistic values flooding the first world. Oscar Handlin expresses a similar view when he remarks as follows:

> The history of immigration is the history of alienation and its consequences. For every freedom won, a tradition lost. For every second generation assimilated, a first generation in one way or another spurned. For the gains of goods and services, an identity lost, and uncertainty found.[3]

Soon after, Srinivas's wife Vasantha succumbs to tuberculosis and dies, leaving him alone. Thus, the dreams of Srinivas of living happily with his family in his 'House No. 5' end as frustrations. The immersion of his wife's ashes into the Thames turns out to be an horrendous experience for Srinivas. The policeman rebukes him for his misdeed—"if everyone carried on the same the river would soon be polluted; the river is not the place for rubbish" (p. 39).[4] Srinivas is left wondering how a flowing river could be polluted by the immersion of ashes. He wrongly identifies the Thames as a substitute for the Ganga, and the policeman's rebukes add insult to his injury.

Time and again, Srinivas suffers from a nostalgia for his homeland that now exists only in his memory. But destiny has something else in store for Srinivas, as he is confronted with a divorcee English woman, Mrs. Pickering, who develops a liking for him. He accommodates Mrs. Pickering in his lonely 'House No. 5', and such is the charismatic effect of this lady that Srinivas, all of a sudden, gladly fixes his identity with England and takes pride in flaunting it. He thinks: "I am becoming more of English than the English, ... and felt almost as if he could enter their skins"(p.69). He does not even object to Mrs. Pickering's cooking meat in his house, even though the very smell of meat chokes him up. He also agrees with Mrs. Pickering's idea of celebrating Christmas in his house, though once he had objected to Sunday being declared as an official holiday, since it had nothing to do with the Indian culture. Markandaya displays how Srinivas surrenders himself to the will of Mrs. Pickering, a quality inherited by the Indians during the civilising mission of the Whites.

Markandaya employs the theme of acculturation and imaginative schizophrenia in the novel under review. She knows from her intimate experience the problems surrounding the diasporic Indians. She makes Srinivas adjust to the western clime and climate, and he proudly utters aloud—'This is my country now.' He is happy to swap his identity with the West, even if it proves to be shortlived. His identity is divided by culture, history and the prevailing circumstances. Made up of Indian clay, he tries to put a layer of Englishness over it and thus tries to become an appropriate man.

Srinivas's father was also a victim of British rule in India. His father was a senior lecturer at a college under the British control, but isolation and racism infected his teaching career immensely, as he was never given company by any Englishmen outside the lecture-room. Unlike his white colleagues, he was not offered any invitation to the Principal's home. His teaching profession taught him the painful lessons of inferiority. To make matters worse, he was declined any promotion to higher posts—'headmaster, principal and vice-chancellor'—which were offered, one after another, to the Englishmen. So, sheer frustration grips him hard and he becomes helpless. Clearly, the father of Srinivas is totally upset over the callous British treatment meted out to him.

The East-West Confrontation hits the novel throughout. In the first part of the novel, this confrontation erupts from the cultural gap, but its victims are often Indians. As Thakur Guruprasad says, "*The Nowhere Man* is a remarkable work of fiction depicting the tragedy of bicultural living in all its harrowing aspects."[5] Colonial barbarism forms a spectre for Srinivas and his family right from his early days. As a young man, he witnesses the confrontation between the Whites and the Indians. A.V. Krishna Rao and Madhvi Menon call this confrontation "not a raucous, raging conflict but a seething and silent one that is eventually resolved by his own efforts".[6] As the violence in colonial India proliferates, and injustice becomes rife, the discontentment and frustation in Indian youth is activated. Srinivas rebels against the British *raj* and plunges into anti-government activities. He tries, as a rebel, to manufacture the petrol bombs with the help of Vasudeva. But this rebellious act hastens Srinivas's departure for England. The police raids Vasudeva's house, and being aware of the horrendous condition on getting held up, he locks himself up in a camphor wood and dies of asphyxation. Vasantha also faces utter humiliation at the hands of policemen. All these racial incidents hasten his immigration to England and there he becomes a 'nowhere man' who has lost his identity. These incidents of his youth recur constantly in his mind when he is in England. That is why M.P. Joseph calls this novel "a documentary on racial prejudice and its origin in colonialism."[7]

However, in the second part of the novel, economic crisis pervading England overtakes this cultural theme, as a result of the disintegration of the British empire caused by the war. Srinivas also suffers economic crisis in his business, deteriorating along with his age. At such a time of crisis, Srinivas's friend Abdul offers him a helping hand and urges him to associate himself in his business, but Srinivas does not accept it. Abdul briefs Srinivas about the England-India relations vehemently:

> Is there no such thing as history? Which tells you how, when they were the top dogs, we were the pariah dogs, only it doesn't spell it out specifically?...Took my land from right under my nose, took my old man first so he

> wouldn't bleat, took my pride so I never walked with my head up, took my freedom finally. (p.75)

The youths of England are hard-pressed with job-crisis, and to worsen the matter immigrants keep on flooding to compete with them in every field. Fred Fletcher and his army of friends—Mike, Joe and Bill—also experience the same sort of job-crisis in their homeland. Such painful is the condition of Fred, an angry young man, that to secure a job for himself he shifts to Australia, where he works as a 'road mender', but dissatisfied with that job he again turns back to England. He has to face the job-scarcity there too. He was a person who, finally switched over to a new place in order to secure a better future. His anger was fuelled by a disclosure from one of his mates that for their present pathetic conditions, "the blacks were responsible. They came in hordes, occupied all the houses, filled up the hospital beds and their offspring took all the places in schools." (p.163). And immediately afterwards, Fred's encounter with the Orientals sparks. First, he tries to harass a black sweeper, telling him "You got no right to be in the country. You bugger off see" (p.164), to which the sweeper retorts: "I got my right when you lot carved up my country" (p.164). Unable to overcome that sweeper, in his next encounter, he throws a coloured youth into the gutter. Carrying on his act of humiliation, he also scolds Srinivas.

Now, Srinivas along with the other blacks faces the wrath of Fred and his fellows. But Srinivas cannot rebel as it will hasten his departure from England and he has nowhere to go. Further, hostility does not have a rational basis:

> BLACKS GO HOME, they said, their fear and hate crystallized into words which opened whole new hells of corresponding fears and desolation in those at whom they were aimed (p.168).

Srinivas, in the meantime, is infected with leprosy, but it doesn't trouble him much. The only thing which bothers him is Fred's outrage against the immigrants settled in England. Fred dislikes the very colour of their skin:

> Fred looked up at him from where he lay. It seemed to him a harmless face, but the colour was wrong. He decided

> that he hated that colour, and the untold evils he and his kind were letting loose in his country....(p.165)

The inexplicable amount of hatred incites Fred to set Srinivas's house on fire, though Srinivas escapes unhurt. Ironically, Fred is burnt to death inside the very house he has set afire. Nemesis overtakes Fred, and in this game of racism the cause of Srinivas is vindicated.

The Nowhere Man, however, is a novel of confrontation rather than of reconciliation between the East and the West. It provides a micro-cosmic view of Indian culture through the life-story of Srinivas and his wife Vasantha (who adheres throughout her life to the 'Indian way of life,' to her *sari*, religion, and rituals). Srinivas's double consciousness is at work in the later part of the novel. He has become an object of isolation, hatred and sometimes of compassion. But that is what the theme of East-West confrontation revolves round and makes the Orient an object, as suggested by Edward Said:

> Orient suitable for study in academy, for display in the museum, for reconstruction in the colonial offices, for theoretical illustration in anthropological, biological, linguistic, racial and historical thesis about mankind and the universe, for instances of economic and sociological theories of development, revolution, cultural personality, natural or religious character.[8]

The Orient as an object is to be seized and exploited at will by the superior power of the Occident. Such a situation, however, willy-nilly leads to a state of confrontation, instead of reconciliation, between the two.

REFERENCES

1. Beson, Evgene and Conoly, L.W. "Kamala Markandaya (1924): Indian Novelist," *Encyclopedia of Post-Colonial Literatures in English*, Volume 2 (London: Routledge, 1994), p. 986.
2. Press, John. ed. *Commonwealth Literature: Unity and Diversity in a Common Culture* (London: Heinemann, 1965), pp. 107-108.
3. http://www.brocku.ca/english/courses lF95immigrant.html.
4. Markandaya, Kamala. *The Nowhere Man* (1972); rpt. Bombay: Orient Longman, 1975), p. 39.

— Subsequent references to this novel will be absorbed in the paper itself.

5. Thakur, Guruprasad. "And Never The Twain Shall Meet: Kamala Markandaya's *The Nowhere Man*", *Language Forum*, Special Issue on Modern Indo-English Fiction, 7, 1-4 (April 1981 - March 1982), pp. 200-1.
6. Rao, A.V.K. *Kamala Markandaya: A Critical Study of Her Novels* (1954-1982). (New Delhi: B.R. Publishing Corporation, 1995), p. 106.
7. Joseph, M.P. *Kamala Markandaya* (New Delhi: Arnold-Heinemann, 1980), p. 73.
8. Said, Edward. *Orientalism*, 1978 (Harmondsworth, England: Penguin, 2001), p. 38.'

Interrogating Canadian Multiculturalism: Bharati Mukherjee's *The World According to Hsü*

7

Nagendra Kumar

Bharati Mukherjee has established herself as the voice of the Indian diaspora in North America. Born into a Bengali-speaking, Hindu Brahmin family in Calcutta in 1940, Mukherjee left India for the University of Iowa in the United States of America in 1962 to pursue an MFA degree. It was there only that she met and married the writer Clark Blaise. In 1966, she followed her husband to his ancestral home of Canada, where they lived, first in Toronto and then in Montreal, as Canadian citizens until 1980. In 1981, Mukherjee and her family left Canada to return to the US, residing in New York until the late 1980s, before they moved to San Francisco, California, where she continues to live and work. Mukherjee became a naturalised US citizen in 1988.

In a critical and creative career that has spanned nearly four decades, Mukherjee has been deeply involved in redefining the idea of diaspora as a process of gain, contrary to conventional perspectives that construe immigration and displacement as a condition of terminal loss and dispossession, concerning the erasure of history and the dissolution of an "original" culture. Attendant with her literary and ideological transcriptions of diaspora, Mukherjee has chosen to describe herself as an "American" writer and has announced through various forums that it is the cultural narrative of America that has provided the enabling site for her own identity transformations as well as those she celebrates in her fictions. Her revisionary cultural politics has aroused considerable critical interest, itself a measure of the author's growing stature.

She has been criticised equally by the US-based India-born critics and the resident Indian critics and reviewers. While the former view her optimistic narration of the American saga of immigrant incarnations as something that elides a consideration of the material realities impinging on Third World immigration, namely, the role of race; class and gender in the workings of identity politics in America (see Roy, Knippling, and Gurleen Grewal) the latter, on the other hand, have taken issue with her negative portrayal of Indian culture and traditions so as to gain the full benefits of Americanisation (see, for instance, Sivaramakrishna). More recent scholars have linked her characters' idealism and assimilation of American culture (with particular reference to the novel *Jasmine*) with her own romanticism about America and her conscious appropriation of American literary traditions (Li 92).

While Mukherjee's professed identity affiliations in the public forum as well as the aesthetic and ideological value of the type of writing she is engaged in, may be heavily invested in her new homeland of America, her literary discourse on nationalism and multiculturalism, does try to grapple with the complexities of national narratives to offer a negotiation that moves beyond a simple acceptance of dominant definitions of national and cultural identity. Like her characters, "with sentimental attachments to a distant homeland but no real desire for permanent return" (Intro. to *Darkness xv*), Mukherjee locates the path of her identity and cultural politics in the course of crossing and recrossing multiple borders of language, history, race, time and culture. Unsettling the constraints and absolutisms of nationalist boundaries, her poetics of diaspora embody her sense of what it means to be a writer who was born and raised in India, been a citizen of Canada and the United States, and who has been shaped and transformed by the cultures of India and North America. Mukherjee herself proclaims her aesthetic stand on the identity reformulations made possible by diaspora as a continuous process of "unhousement" and "rehousement," a process that calls for "breaking away from the culture into which one was born, and in which one's place in society was assured" and "re-rooting oneself in a new culture"(Hancock 39). "In this age of Diasporas," she argues, "one's biological identity may not be one's only identity. Erosions and accretions come with the act of emigration" ("American Dreamer" 4).

Bharati Mukherjee, in the process of 'uprooting' and 're-rooting' had her own share of erosions and accretions. She has admitted, untiringly, how she has undergone identity transformations as she has moved from Canada to the USA. She categorically emphasises a need for cultural citizenship rather than a political one. The idea of cultural citizenship brings into focus the people's emotional ties or psychological experiences of belonging or non-belonging, to the nation. As Katharyne Mitchell asserts that "although immigrants may become legal citizens through a prescribed, state-regulated path, immigrants become cultural citizens only through a reflexive set of formative and locally constructed processes" (emphasis in original, 229). Cultural citizenship takes into consideration the subjective notions of race, ethnicity and otherness in the making of the national narrative of identity and citizenship. Central to cultural citizenship, then, is the idea of difference. The cultural anthropologist Renato Rosaldo argues that cultural citizenship involves the right for people from minority or subordinated groups (recent immigrants, women, members of disadvantaged ethnic groups, etc.) to be different and still belong to the nation. By thus linking culture and citizenship, the fundamental aim cf the discourse of cultural citizenship is to call for "the positive acknowledgment of difference in and by the mainstream" (Miller 2).

Bharati Mukherjee's collection of short stories *Darkness* (1985) consistently interrogates the Canadian concept of multiculturalism and emerges as a radical commentary on that. Especially her stories like "The World According to Hsü", that were written during her stay in Canada, offer a challenge to the dominant paradigms of Canadian multiculturalisms through their implicit call for more fluid or provisional frameworks for the construction of cultural and national identities. Reflecting the author's mood of "unhousement" as a non-white immigrant in Canada, Mukherjee's early stories are pessimistic accounts of rootlessness and despair which depict her immigrant characters as "lost souls, put upon and pathetic [...] adrift in the new world, wondering if they would ever belong" (Intro. to *Darkness* xiii - iv), in contrast to the expatriate whose diligently nurtured "Olympian detachment" ("Imagining Homelands" 73) from the demands and complexities of "rehousement" in the new cultural location confers on him or her necessary insulation from the trauma of exclusion and non-belonging. Mukherjee herself has attributed her representations of South Asian immigrants in Canada to the workings of an "expatriate" sensibility as opposed to the "immigrant" consciousness at work in her later writings (Intro. to *Darkness* xiii, xv). She further elaborates that it is her experience of racism in Canada that is primarily responsible for her cultivation of an attitude of "self-protective irony" and expatriate aloofness in her early works (Intro. to *Darkness* xiv). In "An Invisible Woman," an essay on Canadian racism and multiculturalism, Mukherjee highlights how she was rendered "invisible," on a national and cultural level, by the colour of her skin, a key marker of her visibility as a non-European immigrant. Exoticised as different, but also as inferior, in Toronto and Montreal, she asserts, she was never considered a cultural citizen, *really* Canadian, only a "smelly, dark, alien other" (Connell 12) who threatened to contaminate the white national self. In detailing this "unhoused" phase of her life in her memoir, *Days and Nights in Calcutta*, she voices the anxiety stemming from "the absolute impossibility of ever having a home" (287). In particular, Mukherjee identifies virulent and unabashed racism inherent in the Canadian discourse of multiculturalism as having obstructed the attempts of "ethnic" citizens like her and her characters from staking a claim to a home in the mainstream spaces of the Canadian nation.

Multiculturalism as an official policy was implemented in Canada in 1971, by Prime Minister Pierre Trudeau, as a sign of the nation's commitment to cultural plurality through the accommodation, within the national space, of Canada's ethnically diverse composition, heritage and traditions: its aboriginal peoples, the Anglophone and Francophone groups, the other European immigrants who arrived from the middle of the nineteenth century, and the more recently arrived "visible minority" immigrants from non-European, mostly Asian, countries. However, Mukherjee's contention is that the Canadian multicultural mosaic did not confer cultural citizenship to all of Canada's citizens.

Mukherjee's refutation of thc cultural narrative of the Canadian nation is based on her argument that the terms of liberal multiculturalism, where cultural difference is acknowledged and accommodated within the "mosaic" of national culture, are simply another way of entrenching separateness and marginalising those not recognised as belonging to the dominant culture. The terrorist attack in 1985 on the Air India plane, *Kanishka*, which killed all 300 of its passengers, mostly Canadians of South Asian ancestry, documented in Mukherjee's non-fiction text, *The Sorrow and the Terror,* stands as a harrowing example, according to Mukherjee, of Canada's failure at multiculturalism. What Mukherjee found to be highly upsetting about this incident was that the Canadian government treated the crash as an "Indian" tragedy, the underlying assumption here being that Canadian citizens of Indian origin are not legitimate, not *real*, Canadians.

In "The World According to Hsü," one of the stories written during her period of "unhousement" in Canada and included in the collection, *Darkness,* Mukherjee draws on her experience of the cultural exclusivity of the Canadian nation to explore and express new ways of perceiving Canadian multiculturalism and the national imaginary. Ratna Clayton, one of the story's two central characters, is a Calcutta-born journalist of Indian and Czech descent. Although Ratna is a Canadian citizen and identifies herself as a Canadian, feelings of cultural belonging elude her in Canada. Thus, while "technically" a Canadian, she is aware that she is still positioned as an outsider on account of her "being half — the dominant half — Indian" (*D* 36). In this instance, it is Ratna's darkness of skin, the "visible" marker of her cultural difference that fixes her identity as a foreigner, the national other, in dominant-white Canada: "In Toronto, she was not Canadian, not even Indian. She was something called, after the imported idiom of London, a Paki. And for Pakis, Toronto was hell" (*D* 33).

Mukherjee brings to the fore in the narrative this cultural condition or subjectivity of unbelonging arising from Ratna's experience of racist prejudice in Toronto as a mark of the psychological reverberations of the exclusionary underpinnings of Canadian multiculturalism.

Ratna's husband, Graeme Clayton, is an English-Canadian professor of psychology at a Montreal university. As the story opens, he has been offered a job promotion in Toronto and his chief concern is to persuade Ratna to change her mind and agree to their relocation to Toronto. With this in mind, he takes her for a holiday. Their holiday on an island off the coast of Africa creates the socio-cultural context for Mukherjee's interrogation of the dynamics of Canadian multiculturalism. The island setting itself offers the site for an alternative conception of Canadian citizenship, identity and belonging. The fact that the title of her story alludes to the theory of plate tectonics shows the significance that Mukherjee attaches to it. "Now," says Graeme, reading the article written by the story's eponymous plate tectonics theorist, "Africa and Asia are colliding. India got smashed into Asia... [T]his island is just part of the debris" (*D* 46).

Graeme busies himself on his vacation by carefully cataloguing the differences in the images he sees around him. It is such a binary or static way of thinking about difference that is revealed when we are told that it is through these well-ordered images of "Ektachrome transparency" (*D*30) that Graeme will "entertain and instruct" his friends back home about the world's exotic diversity, its different "genus and species" (*D* 31). Through Graeme's response to his surroundings, Mukherjee articulates a Eurocentric conception of cultural diversity that reveals an absolutist view of cultures. The fact that Graeme is attempting, via his lens, to impose meaning on the "tropical confusion" (*D*30) around him through "a sharpening of line and colour" (*D*32) serves as an analogy for his perception of cultures as orderly and easily definable phenomena, subject to control and containment.

Thus, Bharati Mukherjee seems to suggest that the liberal, state-sanctioned discourse of Canadian multiculturalism is guided by this very view of cultures as fixed, stationery and mutually impermeable. This conception of multiculturalism denies the presence of ambivalence or hybridity through its assertion of superficial pluralism and its belief in the existence of clear boundaries between cultures. In such a "multicultural" nation, differences are organised into neat, virtual grids of distinct ethnic communities, each with its own "culture." Bhabha elaborates:

> [Multicultural policy] entertain[s] and encourage[s] [. . .] cultural diversity, [while correspondingly] containing it. A transparent norm is constituted, a norm given by the host society or dominant culture, which says that these other cultures are fine, but we must be able to locate them within our own grid.
>
> ("The Third Space" 208)

The aim of this model of multiculturalism to control or sanitise cultural difference perfectly calls for the production and preservation of norms and power hierarchies such as margin and centre, insiders and outsiders, us and them. More significantly, this conception of multiculturalism perpetuates the myth of "natural," or "real," difference, from which the discourse of racism gains its pervasive strength.

This kind of consolidation of the dominant discourse of the state, where forms of national identity are exclusionary, homogeneous and unitary, rarely leaves any scope for accommodating, what Mukherjee's narrative suggests, any exchanges, crossings and complex identity "routes" set into play by diaspora, when different groups of people come to live and interact together, sharing one nation.

Thus, while Graeme actively devotes himself "to shap[ing] and reshap[ing] the tropical confusion" (*D*30) of the island's "exotic" terrain, Ratna, in contrast, revels in the unsettled and contingent characteristics of the former colony's cultural constitution: the "Peruvian-looking Africans" (*D*38); the "gaudy paratroopers" patrolling the island; the "black faces from the coast, ubiquitous sentinels among the copper-skinned, straw-hatted natives of the capital" (*D*37). Through Ratna's perception of what appears to her to be the cultural indeterminacy of the island, along with the Indian shops, the nineteenth-century Lutheran churches built by Swedish missionaries, the mission school run by Quebec priests, and the colonial relics of the King's palace and Band, Mukherjee conveys the signs of the complex heterogeneity of national space. It is the ambivalent and mobile configurations of this island's cultural and linguistic constituency that offers Ratna the possibility of experiencing a sense of being "at home" (*D* 48), of attaining the full membership for herself that eludes her in hegemonic-white Toronto.

In this story, then, Mukherjee interrogates Canadian multiculturalism from the perspective of diaspora and the transnational movements and flows of people that have made and continue to make revisions in the discourse of citizenship and national identity necessary. Classified in Canada under the title "visible minority", Ratna Clayton finds herself excluded from the dominant discourse of Canadianness. Half-European and Half-Indian, her darkness of skin is the signifier of the difference which fixes her cultural identity as an Indian or South Asian ethnic, a category viewed to be mutually exclusive with Canadianness. At the end of the story, motley tourists, confined the seedy hotel room due to curfew, dine while sharing with one another their reactions to the happening outside. In the meantime, when her husband defies the curfew and stumbles out to search for the Southern Cross, "She saw the label on the bottle read: 'cote de cassandre'. A superior red table wine that no one had ever heard of...She poured herself another glass, feeling for the moment at home in that collection of Indians and Europeans babbling in English and remembered dialects. No matter where she lived, she would never feel so at home again (*D*48). By thus foregrounding her protagonist's psychological condition of abjection and her experience of racial discrimination, which makes her comfortable even among unknown people at an unknown island rather than in Canada, Mukherjee asks where national subjects of "other" origins locate their home. By invoking the subjective narrative of home and belonging often overlooked by the discourse of formal citizenship and nationalism, Mukherjee suggests that Canadian citizenship needs to be reconceptualised as something that goes beyond the legalistic definition of Canadianness to guarantee a commitment to equality for all subjects, regardless of roots and origins or colour.

REFERENCES

Bhabha, Homi. "The Third Space." *Identity: Community, Culture, Difference*. Ed. J. Rutherford. London: Lawrence and Wishart, 1990.

Connell, Michael, Jessie Grearson and Tom Grimes. "An Interview with Bharati Mukherjee." *The Iowa Review* 20.3 (1990): 7-32.

Hancock, Geoffrey. "An Interview with Bharati Mukherjee." *Canadian Fiction Magazine 59 (1987): 30-44.*

Li, David Leiwei. *Imagining the Nation: Asian American Literature and Cultural Consent.* Stanford: Stanford UP, 1998.

Miller, Toby. "Introducing...Cultural Citizenship." *Social Text* 19.4 (2001): 1-5.

Mitchell, Katharyne. "Transnational Subjects: Constituting the Cultural Citizen in the Era of Pacific Rim Capital." *Ungrounded Empires: The Cultural Politics of Modern Chinese Transnationalism*. Ed. Aihwa Ong and Donald M. Nonini. London: Routledge, 1997.228-56.

Mukherjee, Bharati and Clark Blaise. *Days and Nights in Calcutta*. New York: Doubleday, 1977.

— *Darkness*. New York: Fawcett Cress, 1985.

— "American Dreamer." *MotherJones Magazine* (Jan/Feb. 1997): 1-6.

— "Imagining Homelands." *Letters of Transit: Reflections on Exile, Identity, Language and Loss*. Ed. Andre Aciman. New York: The New Press, 1999. 68-86.

Rosaldo, Renato. "Cultural Citizenship, Inequality, and Multiculturalism." *Latino Cultural Citizenship: Claiming Space, Identity, and Rights*. Ed. William V. Flores and Rina Benmayor. Boston: Beacon Press, 1997. 27-38.

The Problem of Middle Class Woman in the Novels of Shashi Deshpande *The Dark Holds No Terrors, That Long Silence* and *The Binding Vine*

8

Sanjay Kumar Swarnkar

Shashi Deshpande, a leading woman novelist of our time and winner of the prestigious Sahitya Academy Award, depicts a realistic picture of the contemporary middle class family life. Unlike Anita Desai, she is more concerned with the position of women in modern Indian society. She has described the Indian woman as she has seen her in real life, really Indian. All her characters come from the educated middle class. She has got definitely her own point of view as an educated Indian woman of the middle class.

Shashi Deshpande, expresses the woman sensibility in her novels. She is a true Indian English writer who has experienced and studied the problems, frustrations and aspirations of Indian woman of the middle class. Her concern is the urge to find oneself, to create, space for oneself in order to grow on one's own. This paper explores the problems, feelings, experiences and aspirations of the middle class women in her novels.

The Dark Holds No Terrors: It is a novel which explores the myth of man's unquestionable superiority and the myth of woman being a martyr and a paragon of all virtues. It is based on the problems faced by a career woman, a refreshingly new phenomenon in Indian 'English Fiction'.

Sarita or Saru in the daytime is a successful doctor and at night 'a terrified trapped animal' in the hands of her sadist husband Manohar often referred to as Manu, an English teacher in a third rate college. The novel begins with the story of

Saru returning after fifteen years to her father's house, a place she had once sworn never to return but to take care of her father and in reality to escape from the nightmarish brutality of her husband inflicted on her every night.

Her earliest memories are those which underline the discrimination shown by her mother in favour of her brother Dhruva's birthdays.

"Saru recollects how on her brother Dhruva's birthdays, there was always a pooja held in the evenings. She recalls the sense of joyous excitements which pervaded their house on the occasion of his naming ceremony."[1]

This discrimination between the sexes used to upset her. "This obvious form of gender discrimination has been ignored by most writers whose stories one replete with loving and sacrificing mothers, irrespective of the child's gender."[2]

Saru and her mother never used to get along because the mother used to think Saru responsible for the death of her younger brother, Dhruva. Her mother was against Saru's marriage also because Manu was a non-Brahmin. Her mother never praised her "I was an ugly girl. Atleast, my mother told me so. I can remember her eyeing me dispassionately, saying.... you will never be good looking. You are too dark for that."[3]

Against her mother's desire, Saru gets higher education. The discrimination received at the hands of her mother makes her revolt against her parents and seek success in medical college.

"She defies her mother to join the medical college and later she defies her once more to marry out of her taste. In fact, she appears to take a vicious pleasure in deliberately going against her mother's rigid conservatism."[4]

Leaving her two children (Abhi and Renu) at her father's places Saru lives as an isolated, lonely individual, and desires to talk to her father but the unchanging blankness of their relationship saddens her. She thinks that they "are fated to be strangers."[5] Here she recalls the events of her past life, how her brother died, how after the interview by a journalist Manu turned into a sadist and how she used Boozie to gain money and success and he in return used her to cover his homosexuality.

She says, "My husband is a sadist".[6] Her status as a doctor also puts a mark on their relationship.

The brief stay away from Manu and children provides Saru with a chance to review her past, her own psychology, her own place in relation to others in the family and around. With the self-realisation the decision to confront the problem comes "We have to go on trying. If we cannot believe in ourselves, we are sunk."[7] Saru feels that problem exists as much within as outside and so she decides to confront Manu fearlessly, Saru accepts that she is "the guilty sister, the undutiful daughter, the unloving wife...persons spiked with guilts."[8] The novel ends with the assertion of her career and it is here that the significance of the epigraph from "Dhammapada" becomes evident which reads:

"You are your own refuge;
There is no other refuge.
This refuge is hard to achieve."[9]

Through the open ending, it is clear that Saru becomes resolute to control her life by getting rid of her passivity.

The novel taken as a whole, shows a new direction: the assertion of self-dignity. Sarita remains a passive sufferer for a long time but her true self rises from the dark recess like fire. Not losing her female qualities, she rather leaves her husband's home for ever. She learns after fifteen years of trials and tribulations that her strength lies in her own self instead of being a plaything in the hands of men.

The Long Silence: Shashi Deshpande won the Sahitya Academy award for this novel in 1990. Deshpande has narrated a story of contrasting marriage between Jaya and Mohan in this novel. Jaya was named by her father 'Jaya' - for 'Victory' as he used to think of her different from others. Jaya's husband Mohan opted to marry her since she was convent educated and could speak good English. She married him because her elder brother referred to as Dada, had chosen him for her. Mohan who is an engineer, gets transferred to many places. Even he is not shy in using Jaya's uncle's flat at Dadar when they moved to Bombay. It was Dada who first told her about Mohan "He is an engineer....He is quite good looking, no squint, no glasses, even teeth, that's Kamala Kaki. He has a good career, hardworking, ambitious, will go far"—that's Ramukaka... "But determined, you know he will make his way."[10]

After the death of her father, Jaya and her family live at her maternal uncle's place. Jaya's elder brother Dinu goes to America with his wife Gita. Her younger brother Ravi is good for nothing and always quarrels with his wife. He never adheres to any job. "Even as a child, Ravi's lies had been more calculated and pre-meditated than a child's usually are."[11]

At the time of her marriage, Mohan was working at Lohanagar and to please him Jaya started to wear clothes of his choice and had a hair cut like his boss's wife. She even put aside her career as a small writer just to please him. Mohan became involved in a case of malpractice while they were living at their own place at Bombay. At this time, Rahul and Rati were out on a vacation trip with their family friends Rupa and Ashok. Mohan and Jaya shifted to Dadar flat which belonged to Jaya's uncle who was no more in the world. This flat was inherited by Dinu who gave it to Jaya because he was not shifting to India. Jaya kept this secret from everyone, even Mohan. Like Saru of *The Dark Holds No Terrors* and Indu of *Roots and Shadows*, Jaya also is able to reintrospect her life.

Jaya recalls her relationship with Kamat, her neighbour who helps her have her confidence and esteem back and believe in her own individuality. This relationship with Kamat encourages her to make an analysis of her individuality once again and get confidence in her qualities in order to go beyond the social barriers in the pursuit of personal fulfilment. Thus, this relationship imparts an inner fulfilment to Jaya which her relationship with Mohan alone had failed to provide. So it is true that "Kamat's words provide her an insight into the truth about herself and make her accept the responsibility for her deeds."[12]

Kamat agrees to her request of using his address for communication with the editors, "You want to write under a false name?... you want to use my address for your mail? Sure, go ahead!"[13] Thus, he encourages Jaya to write again. But

Kamat dies because of a heart attack. Jaya goes to his flat and sees him lying on the floor. "But I had found him dead-glassy-eyed, foul smelling and dead and—I had walked away from him."[14]

Jaya's maid servant Jeeja, is another typical example of the oppressed woman. She is battered about by her good for nothing drunken husband. Without a murmur of protest, she supports him and even provides him liquor with her hard earned money which she badly needs. She bears no grudge against him even when he takes up another woman. She justifies it by saying: "God did not give us any children—that was his misfortune as well as mine."[15]

Nayana, another maid servant at the Dadar flat is also a victim of this male dominated society. "She had had four children, two girls who lived and two boys who died soon after birth."[16]

Jaya's relations with Kamat were totally on the platonic basis and after the death of Kamat, she comes back to her place without telling it to any one in order to save her marriage.

Mohan at this stage of life wanted full attention of Jaya but as their quarrel continued, suddenly Jaya's outburst of laughter made him angry and so he left the house without saying a single word and did not come back. She feels deserted and an utter loneliness darkness round her. When they come to Dadar flat and Mohan asks for the keys, she ignores his hand and unlocks the gate.

Mohan, her husband, never encouraged Jaya to write and strongly objected to the themes which he suspected to have strong autobiographical overturns. But when she got success, he took pride in the fact of being the husband of a writer. She had relinquished those stories which were taking shape in her, "because I had been scared, scared of hurting Mohan, scared of jeopardising the only career I had, my marriage."[17] "So inspite of her best judgement she gives-up writing fiction and settles down to writing middles to newspaper which pose no problem to anyone."[18]

Jaya's married life has been lived almost on the same lines as the sparrow's. She has built an edifice of security around her husband and children believing it to be a burrow into which she can crawl reptile like and feel safe." His absence unnerves her and she thinks her world will fall apart. But she is hopeful that "Mohan would be back".[19]

Jaya at the same time gets the news from Rupa and Ashok that Rahul has gone away somewhere. She becomes hysterical and she runs from Dadar flat to her own house but in vain. Finally, she gets the information that her son is at Vasant's, her brother-in-law's place, and also a telegram from Mohan that the case has been subsided and all is well. Jaya sees a lot of nightmares in between.

But finally, like Saru and Indu, Jaya too emerges as an individual towards life 'self-confident and having a new perception of life.' She rejects the persistent image of "Two bullocks yoked together".[20] She comes to realise that it is her own self which could break away the bond of subordination and finally she is able to redefine her relation with the world.

The Binding Vine: This novel also throws light on the problems of an educated middle class woman. Like Saru of *The Dark Holds No Terrors* and Indu of *Roots and Shadows*, the heroine of *The Binding Vine* is also a working woman. Whereas Saru is a doctor and Indu is a Journalist, Urmila or Urmi is a lecturer in a college. But unlike them, she is supported by her family even though she got married to the boy next door according to her own wishes.

Urmi's husband Kishore is the elder-step brother of Urmi's best friend Vanaa, i.e. Vandana. He serves in Merchant Navy and is at home only once in a year for a month. Kishore's father married Vanaa's mother for Kishore's sake. His first wife Mira died while giving birth to Kishore. He never loved Vanaa and her mother as he did Kishore and his mother. Whereas Kishore was loved and cared both by Vanaa and her mother and vice versa, Kishore's father was obsessed with his first wife Mira. He saw her at a wedding party and fell in love with her. He made one of his friends suggest his name to Mira's parents and finally they got married. Mira was studying at the time of their marriage. She did not like her husband and he, because 'he' loved her forced himself on her. She got pregnant but had a miscarriage. Though Mira knew that her mother was aware of her situation, they never spoke to each other about this. Like Mohan of *That Long Silence*, Kishore's father too forced himself on her again and again inspite of her unwillingness. Mira was impressed by a poet Venu and used to write poetry like him. Her husband like Mohan stopped her to write. Mira after that used to write in the dark of the night.

Finally, Mira got her freedom when she died. Urmi came to know all of this after many years of her death when Akka (Vanaa's father) told her the story of Mira and gave her the diaries of Mira in which she used to write poems.

Urmi notices the difference in handling over the Mira's property to her. When Akka hands over little bits of Mira's jewellery, she says, "They are Kishore's Mother's ------- I kept them for his wife".[21] But when she hands over the books and diaries of Mira, she says, "Take this, It is Mira's." "She did not mention Kishore at all as if she was now directly linking me with Mira."[22] This shows that a woman loses her identity after her marriage. She is seen either as a wife or mother which in a way erases her real self and imposes another alien self on her. The difference made by Akka symbolises that the poems and diaries are "self-actualising whose identities are not dependent on men."[23]

At the same time, Urmi comes across a woman at the hospital where Vanna used to work as a social worker. That woman Shakutai's daughter Kalpana is brutally raped by someone. Urmi gives mental support to her. There a Doctor Bhaskar Jain falls in love with Urmi. But Urmi ignores this relationship unlike Indu of *Roots and Shadows*. Urmi while going through all this comes to realise pain and suffering of Mira, her dead mother-in-law because, like Kalpana—Mira too was a victim of sexual harassment—a victim of rape in the marriage. Urmi's mother whom she called Inni was not in favour of Urmi helping Shakutai and her daughter as she thought it would put more burden on Urmi's mind since at that time Urmi was mourning for the death of her small daughter Anu. But Urmi made her mother understand the situation and kept on helping Shakutai.

When hospital administration was making Kalpana leave the hospital without becoming conscious, Urmi asked for help from a journalist friend of hers. Due to publicity, the hospital did not shift Kalpana to another hospital and a police enquiry was set.

Suddenly Shakutai's sister Sulu attempted suicide because her husband Prabhakar never used to touch her due to her skin disease. Prabhakar wanted Kalpana to be his wife. Sulu who was the perfect house keeper and used to take care of Shakutai's children because her husband used to live with another woman, had to compromise with the situation just to have so-called security of a marriage. But Kalpana because of her refusal, becomes a victim of Prabhakar's obsession. Finally, one day he got the chance to fulfil his obsessive desires successfully. Sulu even tried to persuade Kalpana to marry her uncle so that she could at least continue to stay in the house. She feared that if Prabhakar took some other women, she would become a destitute. But, later on she immolates herself when she comes to know that her husband raped Kalpana.

Shakutai who first used to worry that even her younger daughter too would not get a husband, asks Urmi whether she should inform the police about Prabhakar. Urmi tells her to take her own decision and empowers Shakutai. Urmi also takes the decision of having Mira's poetry publish and give a voice to her.

To sum up, it can be said that it is significant in the creative female world of Deshpande, all men are not villains. The husband of the protagonist Urmi is good to her and she is fully satisfied with him. But she feels the responsibility to her own creed the 'Strijati' and struggles to bring its truth before the society.

Shashi Deshpande gets to the root of existence through her female characters. Male or female, there is a division within ourselves that leads us to love and hate to be gentle and good and at the same time becomes an agent of cruelty. This is the message of this novel. Human nature is the "hardest to bridge, the hardest to accept, to live with."[24]

Thus, we see that Shashi Deshpande has particularly concentrated on the typical dilemma of middle class educated and employed Indian women whose problems are different from those of urban women in India. She has her own independent views on women, their position and predicament, their trials and tribulations which deserve a careful consideration and evaluation. She knows intimately the segment of Indian society about which she writes and can easily empathise with it.

Many of her characters are persons who are frustrated either sexually or professionally. Her novels generally centre round family relationships particularly the relationship between husband and wife and latter's dilemmas and conflicts. According to her, everybody especially a woman, has to live within relationship and there is no other way.

The message of Deshpande's writing is limited and it covers only the problems belonging to the middle class women in the Indian context. Though the scope of her thinking is confined and focuses on the individual's natures only, she seeks all the solutions in the context of the Indian society. The protagonists of Shashi Deshpande start a campaign but in the end they realise that the solutions can be found at the best within the confines of the Indian Society. Her endeavours ensure a base of consistency for the Indian middle class women. As a whole, the attempt and presentation of Deshpande is admirable and her writing has got a message for middle class Indian women to grow on in the society of which they are important members.

REFERENCES

1. Y.S. Sunita Reddy. "You are your own refuge: The Dark Holds No Terrors:" *A Feminist Perspective on the Novels of Shashi Deshanpde*, (New Delhi: Prestige, 2001), p. 49.
2. *Ibid.*, p.51
3. Shashi Deshpande. *The Dark Holds No Terrors*, (New Delhi: Penguin Books, 1990), p.61.
4. Y.S. Sunita Reddy. "You are your own refuge: The Dark Holds No Terrors:" *A Feminist Perspective on the Novels of Shashi Deshanpde*, (New Delhi: Prestige, 2001), p. 55.
5. Shashi Deshpande. *The Dark Holds No Terrors*, (New Delhi: Penguin Books, 1990), p.105.
6. *Ibid.*, p. 199.

7. *Ibid.*, p. 220.
8. Seema Suneel. "Marriage, A Compromise: A Study of Shashi Deshpande:" *The Dark Holds No Terrors: Man Woman Relationship in Indian Fiction* (New Delhi: Prestige, 1995), p. 113.
9. From the Dhammapada, quoted at the beginning of the novel, *The Dark Holds No Terrors.*
10. Shashi Deshpande. *That Long Silence* (New Delhi: Penguin Books, 1989), pp. 91-92.
11. *Ibid.*, p. 101
12. Rashmi Gaur. "That Long Silence: Journey Towards Self Actualization:" *Women in the Novels of Shashi Deshpande* ed. by Suman Bala, N.D. Khosla Publishing House, 2001, p. 95
13. Shashi Deshpande. *That Long Silence*, p. 146.
14. *Ibid.*, p. 157
15. *Ibid.*, p.52
16. *Ibid.*, p. 27
17. *Ibid.*, p. 144
18. Rajeshwar Mittapalli. "The Traum of a Housewife: Shashi Deshpande's *That Long Silence." Shashi Deshpande: A Critical Spectrum*, ed. by T.M.J. Indra Mohan, New Delhi, Atlantic, 2004, p. 68.
19. *That Long Silence*, p. 127.
20. *Ibid.*, p. 191.
21. Shashi Deshpande. *The Binding Vine* (New Delhi: Penguin Books, 1993; rpt. 2001), p.48.
22. *Ibid.*, p. 48.
23. Wendy Martin. "The Female Mystique in American Fiction," *Female Studies* II ed. Howe p. 83.

    Quoted by Veena Noble Das, "Feminism and Literature," *The Commonwealth Review*, Vol. VI No.1, 1994-95, p. 10
25. *The Binding Vine*, p. 201.

Nobel Laureate Jelinek's *Signatures*: Truth or Pornography?

9

Neeru Tandon and Kavita Shukla

Born in 1946, a child of the Jewish origin, Jelinek was educated in a convent school, later on earned an organist's diploma at the celebrated Vienna Conservatory. Due to an anxiety disorder, her University course in drama was interrupted. Meanwhile, her father had been shut up in a mental asylum. All these tensions led Jelinek to the withdrawl from life and an openness to face it too. This contradictory situation prepared the platform for the key themes in Jelinek's works. Her themes are brutally open in exposing, particularly a woman, to every kind of exploitation, degradation, and violence. In an interview with German writer Hans-Jurgen Heinrichs, she explains, "Mine is a social intelligence that does not derive from knowledge and experience, but from avoiding them."[1] It is tremendously encouraging for all the readers who dare to read daredevil, that Elfriede Jelinek won the Noble Prize for Literature in 2004. All her writings *Lust, Women As Lovers, The Piano Teacher, Wonderful, Wonderful, Times* and *Greed* are full of tireless fury with the human race.

About *Greed*, Philip Roth says that the novel is dead, but I would advocate that we the readers are dead. We are too dependent on a sensible, smells-good fiction, prose and fantasy. We forget that hard-core writing is not about rules. It's about the dynamic sense of survival against the odds.

Jelinek's work is brave, risky and antagonistic. In America, she has been absurdly criticised for writing porn, but they forget that she is not a moral philosopher, she is a novelist and she has the right to be provocative and voicing unpleasant. She combines the highly cultivated literary styles with political concerns.

If we speak about porn writing, it could be defined as—writing intended to provoke feelings of lust in the reader, and contains less literary value. From a definite standpoint, pornography is anything that is created to cause sexual excitement or arousal. Although women's bodies are the final destination of adult pornography, we cannot bypass the child pornography, gay pornography, and animal pornography. Hence I define pornography as the exposure of genitals with sexual degradation and abuse in a manner that endorses and encourages the sexual stimulation in the male characters.

After reading the five novels of Jelinek, I could analyse that each one is more unpleasant than the one before, and all denunciate the still patriarchal Austrian society. In an aggressive tone, the novel *Greed* portrays the social dimensions in which the woman is used as an attire to be used and thrown into the gutter, to be exploited both sexually and socially. Kurt Janisch, the typical of Jelinek's men, the policeman, symbol of patriarchal society, is violent, insatiable and possess a greed for domination. Kurt, who goes about sex with Gerti, only wants to get hold of her property; this is the ultimate object of her greed, and the novel superimposes the image of the house with the image of the body. He prostitutes himself to every woman in the vicinity and beyond, in the hope that they will hand over their property to him one day. He looks at female genitalia in the way as if these doors are permanently open for him. Sex is furtive and base—**"you give each other a good licking"**—and love is a common foible, which, for women at least, involve a dangerous loss of selfhood. What women want from their men is neither gentle nor soft nor reasonable—it is just true.

The novel *Women As Lovers* was published in 1975. The book presents a group of young characters uncritically adopting the shallow money-driven conventions that, as Jelinek sees it, regulate sex and marriage in provincial Australia. Jelinek has unremittingly established her genius throughout this work of fiction, she doesn't even spare a moment to satirise the hypocrisy that is as evident in today's world as sunshine itself. She has truly brought out the ignominious life of the married women in her native nation. However, this description applies equally well to nearly all the geographical boundaries across the globe. She has also given a picture of all those who were silenced prematurely, thus giving a serious jolt to the Almighty's concept of an ideal co-existence between men and women.

"I love you so much, says brigette. My gleaming hair supports my love. What also supports my love: your job, which has a future. What supports my love apart from that: I myself, who have nothing at all."

This solitary portrayal itself suffices for the Platonic Love that encapsulates the very subsistence of one the striving protagonists of The Award-embracing oeuvre of the celebrated Austrian novelist Elfriede Jelinek. In this magnum opus of hers, she has artistically depicted the tranquil tornadoes that rest inside the very perturbed-self of the aforementioned compatriot of the instigator herself. Barring all the elements of proficiency that are so evident in her novels, there is yet a non-failing rudiment of the truest possible portrayal of ugliness that enshrouds the state of most of the contemporary women, chiefly of those who dwell in the murkier dimensions of the society; regardless of their nationality. Her acrid courtesies towards the predominant sex depict her as a cynic and misanthropist; however that's just a trifle of a response—for there's never enough stock of gunpowder in the arsenals of even her staunchest critics. She is just exquisitely celestial when her genius is concerned. And being an esteemed Nobel Laureate itself says it all.

In this distinguished sonata of hers, she has epitomised the pinnacle of love that a woman can have for someone she adores from the cores of her bosom. The protagonists of the novel are christened Brigitte and Paula, the daredevils who strike with the might of a tornado when it comes to their respective fiances, in their own signature ways. Brigitte is the entity more subjugated of the two, who sews brassieres, she is truly apt at this art of hers; but it doesn't take her even cinch of a second to hope that **"Heinz will get her out of here."** She worships her man; she looks at her with all the respect she can muster from her devastated inner self. Her love is indeed true, for her cravings and yearnings proclaim her sentiments. Heinz is the soul-saving grace of ignominous life. Prolific drams of pathetic whirlwinds of the dark morass of apprehension continue to rock her trembled-self with a constant momentum. For Brigitte, Heinz means everything. Basically, Brigitte is portrayed as a dismal soul who attaches little self-worth to her. She is devoid of all measures of confidence and pride that the Almighty would have loved to instill in her. She herself hails from an obscure-sounding place that yields a low-profile "factory": it is this very factory that accounts for the continuation of her otherwise extremely wretched life. But her dreams are far from being the viewpoint of the victims—but rather from those of the observers; she comments on the mutual traitors in the two extreme boundaries of genders and in this way she pronounces her own satirical decrees on the prevalent political developments. Through her text, she wants to reveal what is and has been concealed. She has pointed out the fallacy of the society in order to make us use our privileged acumens instead of the rancid idiosyncrasy that is so rampant in today's configuration of the general public. She has been constantly striving to devise and proclaim a Nobel criterion for the feminine gender, and thus, we all would be able to give a wide berth all the established canards that ridicule the female subsistence; a new order which is only conceivable through aggressive use of brutal forces.

In the lecture that she delivered the evening she was awarded The Nobel, she asserted that it "shamelessly rolls around under the hands of the caressers", then she was truly petrified on learning that the language has been disarmed and has lost much of its sheen, thus it has also been robbed of its might. She was under acute peril of being dragged into the 'culture machine' and thus being untrue to her upright vocation as a writer. She battles against the temptation of the language to make itself "the slave of stranger's hand, no matter how good it feels." However, the reaction of the oppression involved in the stereotypical images is not, and cannot ever be, limited to protests. The important task that much of Afro-American and feminist literary as well as critical efforts engage with us the construction of an authentic subjectivity. It is in this very context that Man is always considered as a significant text and subjectivity. It itself is a highly problematic concept in all forms of contemporary critical discourses, and it is important to put it in correct perspective there. Jelinek as a feminist, opposes the patriarchal notion of a unilateral self, is attempting to forge a unified, coherent and gender defined identity for women; but as a matter of fact, women writers have not yet experienced that subjectivity which will give them a sense of personal autonomy, continuous identity, a history and an agency in the world. In fact, yet so far feminists have got the success only to deconstruct the myth of as the absolute other and expose it as a position within a patriarchal discourse. Moreover, the need to challenge gender stereotypes has led scores of women writers and feminists to examine identity in relational terms, rather than as a unitary, self-directing and isolated ego.

In Jelinek's *Women as Lovers*, one can easily see the complex operations of the possibility and denial of self in terms that are essentially rational. The gradual discovery of Paula's permeability is linked with the narrator's sense of identity. The invisibility is exactly not the biochemical accident to her epidermis; it is because of a peculiar disposition of the eyes of those for whom a female is not a matter of identity. She pines throughout the span of the novel to give voice to her subsistence, as being invisible itself implies being formless. Jelinek has unearthed the division of society along the lines of race and gender. The author, in her agonised recitation of the sorry expeditions of the protagonists, has discovered the possibility of authentic identity of women and projects the women characters through the balanced perception. Through her writings in the most oppressive moods, the esteemed instigator has stated that a woman is merely an object of cosmopolitan ridicule and her entire existence is devastated, her never-failing hope makes her trudge on her gloomy path, until she discovers dawn. And dawn she does discover; she does get it right.

However, the world is not all that rosy for Paula, another protagonist in the novel. She lives in countryside with a small family of hers that comprises of her irate father, her timid. mother and her merciless brother. Paula is an adorable, yet not beautiful lass who is in her early teens. It is told that by this age, the girls are asked to dwell their (already overwhelmed) brains on the most serious note of their slaughtered life-regarding "what she wants to be one day: housewife or sales assistant." Paula cries off both—rather shuns them off. She wants to make a mark of her life by "learning dressmaking"—an intention that her petrified mother considers highly parabolic to the established canards. Plus, her mother is perhaps not the most suitable candidate to be chided, for she does want to keep her adorable darling away from all sorts of perils that will she might trade for this enterprising aspirations of hers. She herself remarks,

> "When my dada was still alive, I slaved for him, and then went on slaving for your dada and Gerald, and now that you're old enough to me, you suddenly don't want any more but learn the clean trade of dressmaking instead. Why and for what have I slaved all my life, if not for dada and Gerald, and now you could at last slave with me, you don't want to. You can put it out of your head! Before dada and Gerald put it out of your head for you."[3]

Even though she is dwelling dangerously in such morbid and oppressive state of affairs, Brigitte's resilience refuses to lie low. Thus "... paula goes on looking at the better world." Whether it's her better luck or her conviction that she is allowed to have her final say in this debacle, she is allowed to move to the nearby town to learn dressmaking, albeit some restrictions are also put on her to curb her free sailing. Her fervour sees her through of all formative shortcomings of her beautiful life.

The aftermath of any audacious inference that any uncouth fragile soul derives, is furthered by her instigators—and this time the remuneration consists of some terrible for the recipient's dinner. It's all quite terrible to any civilised society, but alas, there is no such society when it comes to the fragile sex. They have been subjected to inhumane torture, brutal afflictions and even their existence is put to the sword—this is not done to prove the supremacy of the prominent gender over the plagued one, but is rather done only to establish this pathetic truth. To scale such indeed glorious accolades, even rape and bloodbath is of little concern. Jelinek has tried to put up a forlorn question: God produced us both, so we worship Him; but how can one consider us inferior to the other gender when we alone are capable of giving birth? Not only do you people stereotype us as inferior, you also make us feel wretched—just because you have physical strength that we don't seem to possess? It takes guts to give birth to someone and it is one hell of a respectable job, akin to the Almighty Himself, yet you pathetic mean sacks think that's the way "with these doormats!" Your mother fed you on her milk, your sister fed you on her blood and your daughter will feed you with her life, yet your way of thinking is so dismal that can't even foresee our vitality! Where would you be if there would be no mothers to give birth, no sisters to cater and no daughters to feed you? Indeed it'll throw our system out of balance, yet please do spare a thought or two for as well...

> "life seems meaningless without him, even with him life doesn't seem to be very meaningful, at any rate more meaningful than her work in the brassiere factory".
>
> "come back, heinz! I love you, and I need you".[4]

These heart-wringing cries symbolise the helpless love of Brigitte, who is perhaps the self-proclaimed spokesperson of the instigator herself. Jelinek has drained the lion's share of her privileged acumens to produce this one scintilla of a line—wherein she exhibits her earnest yearnings for the man she loves. Her effort is still more commendable in the light of the horrible state of affairs that enshroud her co-protagonist's entire being. Jelinek has illustrated that she does have those unique sparks in her creations that trigger-off a high voltage response for her uneasy stimuli. She has dared to take her soul to these people who are marginalised and downtrodden; and thus, like a thermometer, taken a bit of the oppressive heat that those poor souls face everyday and every night. The passion, the fervour, the authenticity with which she has blasted-off the prevalent assertions that women can never be a part of literary texts is commendable.

Claiming one's identity or writing about one's admonished self in order to inculcate and launch a sense of self-worth is extremely crucial elements and thus, is Jelinek's *Signatures*. Her idiosyncrasy regarding the dismal rather wretched environment in which her protagonists dwell, questions the reader in his very face: how do you feel now and how would you have felt had the very same things happened to your mother or your sister or your daughter? This one question is found zeroing-in on the reader's subconscious psyche and Jelinek's feminism makes one ponder over the "in attendance" conditions of the women, globally. What if we're cooling our heels in our homes and excusing ourselves from any such botheration, these issues are, nevertheless, staring at us fixatedly. The immaculate polarity of authority distribution has been marring the configuration of our civilised society since time immemorial; it is so damn wrong, yet no one sees it. Men consistently need some poor soul to exercise their authority on: this satisfies their ego: and women are the most suitable candidates for the purpose—for they are timid, or worse, they can be made timid (by slashing their integrity first as an individual, followed by blasting-off their feminine subsistence). That's exactly where Jelinek has been so good at: her denial of stereotypical destructive versions of fragility, infested in her contemporary women, is emphasised on the grounds of sexuality, breakdowns and challenges to the self-esteem posed by the negative versions of women's beauty "like a sponge which has never squeezed out." This implication can be furthered by considering the author's expertise as a triangle; the surface of which emblazoned by attacking language, and the three corner points approach three distinct courses—towards a feminist perspective, a Nazi past and the last one, the political arena—and every angle of the triangle itself thunders like a hailstorm following a controversial attitude.

The thematic and linguistic multiplicity of her novels continues to shine with dazzling brilliance in her plays too. She does not view the war from confined to provide sexual gratification only. Thus, the belief that "a woman's claim to the rights of creation means first to create self," itself lays emphasis on finding a separate entity in which a woman has to build herself up psychologically even before for right is placed before the society. The question of self is more of a matter of understanding than fulfilment. Jelinek's portrayal of women is an antagonising set of the social as well as political values. She has attained popularity not only for writing literature with female protagonists but also for projecting the true woman who, de facto, remains in the background. This implies that an ideal woman is not the woman whom she has described, but the woman as it is, and ought to be. The serious issue is that in the projection of mind, soul or the physical entity a 'being'; the inner self is never represented. The reality claims that a human being is divided into so many sleeves among whom it becomes troublesome to say as to which self must be the real one.

In *Lust*, Jelinek has illustrated the debacles, the fiascos and their aftermath that run the life of the bleakest creature that ever treaded this Planet. Gerti, the timorous yet audacious, protagonist of the oeuvre is the unfortunate spouse of Hermann, who "...sings, plays, yells, fucks." Everyday sun rises, with it; raise the hardships of hers that can alone suffice to bring even the Satan to ignominy. Hermann is merely a lesser mortal who is "just a fart in hurricane", and has got just one philosophy to take care of: "it doesn't take long to make merry." Gerti is analogous to a receptor antenna that is bound to the receiver's appalling frequencies that are the habitual springs of inexcusable treatments, whose description even one may regard as grisly. The badly bruised Gerti, then one day, "bares her soul and her bosom with words", to Michael, who didn't went "astray" when it came to rescue her from her regular butcher. That was a day when her esteemed, yet undermined feminism, was put to the extreme batteries. A thoroughly battered soul, amalgamated with a dilapidated physical realm, better known as Gerti, surrendered all that she had to her saviour. And this pristine operation should not be considered from the point of view of her perfidy, but rather by perceiving that a soul as pure as crystal rain, was asked to emanate from a chunk of charcoal. However, there is still no respite for this poor soul Gerti as Michael, too, is another brute of the same genre as that of Hermann. Devastated and shattered Gerti is left to cry for herself.

"When she bends down she has to spread her legs. Now he can cop hold of her whole fig tree with one hand and set his fingers angrily a-roving. Oh and while she's at it with her legs apart like that she can stand over him and piss him in his mouth."[5]

The signature approach of Elfriede Jelinek towards one of the nuts and bolts of all living beings, humans and brutes alike, sex has been more of deference as an art than anything else. She is truly well verse at this elucidation of hers—for she doesn't consider it forbidden to air her revered analysis regarding this audacious subject. She has very artistically depicted the terrible music that scores of her contemporary women have to face everyday. They are taken as wives only for one principle cause: sexual gratification. These wretched, pathetic, dismal creatures are perhaps deserted by the Almighty also—for they are simply forsaken in His kind Kingdom, with nothing to help their undermined souls, that renders them subjugated.

"The woman is passive as a toilet, for the man to do his business in. He shoves her head into the bathtub and, his hand clawing her hair, threatens that as you make your bed, so you must cry on it, that's love. No, cries the woman. She isn't crying for love."[6]

These sorry tales determine the diluted nerves and murky equations that they have to face day-in and day-out. The protagonist of this novel is no different, at least in the terms of the ghastly courtesies that are always at her disposal because of her husband. Her spouse "is as puffed-up as a pig's bladder, he sings, plays, yells, fucks." Murkier become all the dimensions of one's life when one has a spouse who is so focused with the vision of one's life! Almost instantaneously, one is strained by an unnatural stimulus to think if for such a fanatically determined spouse, the one at the receiving end is a woman! A meek woman, that is, very politely, the meekest creature Almighty ever created. Sorry tales trail...

Throughout the length and breadth of this opus of hers, Jelinek has portrayed that Gerti is as "passive as a toilet, for the man to do his business in." Alarms emblazon her morbid-sounding wails, yet she is desperate to vent her agony out. And she discovers Michael the most suitable candidate for the same, after her entire revered someone who only yells razes feminine-self. Jelinek has astonishingly verified the pinnacle of her scholarly insight in this mesmerising sonata to illustrate Gerti's affliction and her pining and yearnings for freedom; freedom from regular rapist, who happens to be her spouse also. Marital rape is but one instance of Gerti's abuse, she is pressed to pose the ultimate ridicule of her crushed subsistence in more ways than one. "The woman has to crook and angle her legs like a frog so that her husband, the examining magistrate, can look into the matter closely."[7] Not only this, she is forced to oblige him in all the ways she is ordered to, viz. "He stares at her cleft. This is familiar territory now. When she looks away, because she cannot bear his scrutiny and the groping, pinching hands that examine her, he hits her. He wants to see and do everything. He has a right to. There are details you can't see, and, in the event of there being a next time, a flashlight would come handy."[8]

Aforesaid arguments sponsor a useful and a pretty obvious inference that there are only two distinct ways in which one can dehumanise a woman to such extremes that her entire subsistence, including her feminism is all razed. And these ways are superseded by everything else—they are pornography and marital rape. However, there does exist a subtle distinction between the two; whereas pornography is more centred on the grounds of financial and/or sexual securities, marital rape sabotages the entire being of a woman for merely ego-satisfaction of a sadist. Such a sadist is under a two-way reprimand from the Almighty—for the culprit is not only inflicting pain on someone's physical domains, but also he is viciously piercing her tender spirits.

The Piano Teacher sets up an unusual triangular power struggle. Despite dwindling energies, an ageing mother tries to keep her pianist daughter away from men, her ambition having been to "squeeze money out of [her daughter's] arduously achieved perfection."[9] Erika the piano teacher, is as it were hypnotised by the sexual experience that has passed her by. She dresses unsuitably in youthful dresses and stays out late after her lessons, but perhaps to provoke her mother and cultivate the illusion of a freedom she doesn't have or even truly want. Into this stale scenario steps a young piano student, Walter Klemmer, determined to add his list of conquests.

In particular, the novel has two scenes of great dramatic effect where actions, dialogue, and reflection work powerfully together. The first is in the school bathroom where the vigorous, sporty Klemmer boldly kisses his ageing sleeping beauty into life; Erika enjoys a moment of abandonment, then transforms this opportunity for passion into a frustrating masturbation scene in which the man, as if being taught a lesson, is brought to orgasm, then forced to recompose himself.

Some days later, back home, Erika barricades herself in her room with Klemmer and forces him to read a letter in which she begs him to mistreat her, beat her, tie her up, and so on.

Such an account of the book suggests a familiar kind of unhappy psychological drama, but Jelinek's prose has now abandoned the transparency of the conventional novel.

The Piano Teacher is a repentant tale of two mutually conflicting philosophies and their habitual divergence. Curtailed liberty of spirits and reciprocally hyper-parabolic polarities of the respective idiosyncrasies of the protagonist and her tyrannical mother are the hallmarks of this scintilla of Jelinek. She has very ardently brought out the congestion of ideologies between a mother and her kid; and also the tidal waves of unrest that punctually keep on rocking the seaboards of the ever tranquil ocean of never failing timidity of her prodigious kid, orthogonally christened as Erika Kohut. Payable to the never deterring courtesies of her mother, Erika and her festival spirits have undergone mutation—while Erika is more of a frostfish that is devoid of all drams of self-love; her mother is more of a counterpart of hers, say, a swordfish—who regularly devours on the suppleness of her daughter's soul. "Mother can't always prevent Erika from buying something, but she can dictate what Erika puts on. Mother is an absolute ruler."[10] So ghastly is mother's repute that the reader is, almost instantaneously, magnetised to a polarity exactly contravening hers.

The Piano Teacher follows Erika as she moves away from the entrapment of her monster mother and steps into her own metaphorical private room, replacing their bond by forming a new relationship with one of her young male students. She moves from the designation of a strict, sadistic professor demanding immediate obedience from her student to a domain where her own passion, hidden and sick desires to be submissive and abused by the same student finally undoes her.

"Time passes, and we pass the time. They are enclosed together in a bell jar: Erika, her protective hulls, her mama. The jar can be lifted only if an outsider grabs the glass knob on the top and pulls it up. Erika is an insect encased in amber, timeless, ageless. She has no history, and she doesn't seem to make a fuss. This insect has long since lost its ability to creep and crawl. Erika is baked inside the cake pan of eternity. She joyfully shares this eternity with her beloved composers, but she certainly can't hold a candle to them when it comes to being loved."[11]

Much of the melodrama that encapsulates this pinnacle of an illustration that concerns a submerged subsistence of a disastrous ascendancy of her personal resources by a teacher herself is what one better discerns as *The Piano Teacher*, the unveiling marvel of Austria's most favoured pen chanter—Elfriede Jelinek. The celestial mysticism that has been the hallmark of all her literary exploits, commencing from this very magnum opus usually revolves around a subjugated and overwhelmed distinctiveness; usually it's a fictional account of one of her compatriots. In this oeuvre of hers too, Jelinek has portrayed how an utterly acrid and symbiotic liaison of a prodigy kid with her fixatedly totalitarian mother results in the ultimate dehumanisation of human values of the former. Even Sadomasochistic attitude becomes evident in the protagonist's sub-conscious as is pretty obvious in the atrocious manner she attempts to put herself to bleeding recurrently.

Jelinek reveals deeper and more threatening movements toward rebellion. Erika has dark sexual urges. She visits a Turkish peep show beneath a bridge in a sluggish part of Vienna to catch a glance of live porn shows where she is the only non-doer around. Later she is seen in the hidden parts of town where she watches uncivilised sadomasochistic movies and spies the nude and dangerous world of lovers in the late night.

The conflict between the two mutates Erika's gentle self to a sadist, and this is illustrated by a few instances that Jelinek has depicted. Erika is now all prepared to make all the ridiculous and tyrannical fantasies of her despotic mother: she spends

Thomas Bernhard, who had also remorselessly attacked the residual fascism of modern Australia; Jelinek claims that as a man Bernhard "could claim a position of authority," projecting an identity with which the readers could relate and give a coherent, convincing account of Austrian society whereas being a woman even this form of "positive" approach was denied to her.

I would like to support the view that pornography is self-evident or entirely in the eyes of the beholder. Researches show that there is no consensus on how to define pornography and it would be difficult to summarise that whether or not a pornographic label to any case or creation is appropriate. Pornography, therefore, should not be a subject to legal restraint, or even opprobrium. What is objectionable about pornography is its abusive and degrading portrayal of females and female sexulity, not its sexual contents. If we analyse Jelinek deeply here, we come with the firm point that the burning history of Nazi past compels her to be so provocative. Jelinek's fury against the male dominant patriarchal society, and the torture, mutilation, injury and pains of real women, which was a matter of sexual pleasure to the male order, appears with more explosive forces in her writings. I agree that the language may be bare and tough nude but the agony of Austrian women is nuder and Jelinek's writing is an attempt to reveal the layers of that barbaric history. Either it is the poor Gerti of *Lust* or the rich Gerti of *Greed*, either we talk about the marvellous talent Erika or the low profile Paula, each of them is portrayed finally as the object of sexual gratification for the male society. And this is the concern of the writer for the wretched condition of fairer sex. She makes us to feel pathetic about ourselves, to feel pity about our tragic condition and she finally provokes us to say a bold no to the oppressions of male dominance. If all these efforts declare her a porn writer, then being porn is a matter of literary worth as per my estimation.

WORKS CITED

1. Hans-Jurgen Heinrichs. 'Interview with Elfriede Jelinek,' in the book *Schreibenist das bessere Leben: Gesprache Mit Autoren* [Munich: Kunstmann, 2006], 21.

2. Elfriede Jelinek. *Women as Lovers* [London: Serpent's tail, 1994], 25.
3. *Ibid.*, 18.
4. *Ibid.*, 24.
5. Elfriede Jelinek. *Lust* [London: Serpent's tail, 1992], 35.
6. *Ibid.*, 33.
7. *Ibid.*, 65.
8. *Ibid.*, 102.
9. Elfriede Jelinek. *The Piano Teacher*, [London: Serpent's tail, 1989], 8.
10. *Ibid.*, 14.
11. *Ibid.*, 42.
12. *Ibid.*, 80.
13. *Ibid.*
14. *Ibid.*, 81.

Bharati Mukherjee's *Jasmine*: A Saga of Alienation and Exile

10

Sanjit Mishra

"The man who finds his homeland sweet is still a tender beginner; he to whom every soil is as his native land is already strong; but he is perfect to whom the entire world is a foreign land."

- Hugh of St. Victor, 12th century

"Exile is the unhealable rift forced between a human and a native place, between the self and its true home: its essential sadness can never be surmounted. The achievements of exile are permanently undermined by the loss of something left behind forever."

- *Edward Said,* Reflections on Exile

Ever since the Fall of Man as a result of.. .the first Disobedience / And the fruit...whose mortal taste brought / Death unto this world...." (Milton, *Paradise Lost, Book I*) the humans have been living in this world in a state of Universal Exile. In the last one hundred years, displacement and exile have become the common fate of groups and individuals too numerous to mention as the ravages of totalitarianism, genocidal ideology, fundamentalism and nationalism have bereft scores of communities of their homes and homelands. The modern world, on account of an unprecedented rise in scientific and technological advancements in every walk of life, appears to have shrunk into a virtual global village. The 21st century is witness to an altogether new phenomenon of inter-cultural and inter-racial awareness among men and women over the world. The resultant cultural mixing in this postcolonial era has generated a sort of hybrid culture. To quote Bill Ashcroft et al:

"Postcolonial culture is inevitably a hybrid phenomenon involving a dialectical relationship between the grafted European cultural systems and an indigenous ontology, with its impulse to recreate or create an independent local identity. Such construction or reconstruction occurs as a dynamic interaction between European hegemonic and peripheral subversions of them" (p. 195).

It is equally fruitful to note that the capitalist forces of the West, chiefly led by America have brought forth a drastic shift in The cultural patterns the world over. To quote Frederic Jameson:

"Post modern culture is the internal and super structural expression of a whole new wave of American military and economic domination throughout the world: in this sense, as throughout class history, the underside of culture is blood, torture, death and terror."

Significantly, it is this so called "American Dream" that has been attracting people from across the world and many young men and women feel drawn to this country for a variety of economic and other considerations. This intermingling and interaction between different cultures, however is not smooth enough, nor always fruitful. It has its own scars and disenchantments in the case of those whose experiences in a cross-cultural interface are not very healthy. This paper attempts to trace the cultural ramifications in Bharati Mukherjee's novel *Jasmine* (1989).

Thinking of home is often accompanied by nostalgia, the absence or loss of loved ones, the remoteness of the home one is cut off from. As a matter of fact, we are all "exiles" from our past, our childhood, and of course, that universal "home". The state of exile, the pain of separation and disorientation makes Bharati Mukherjee's novel *Jasmine* a quest for identity in an alien land. Bharati Mukherjee has eloquently succeeded in creating a kind of impressionistic fable, a prose poem, about being an exile, a refugee, and a spiritual vagabond in the world today. *Jasmine* was generally received enthusiastically, but there was some criticism that it was too short and its plot too contrived to be a really successful work of fiction. It is a novel that stems from an earlier short story from *The Middleman and Other Stories* and was expanded to a story of a young widow who uproots herself from her life in India and re-roots herself in search of a new life and the image of America. It is a story of dislocation and relocation as the title character continually sheds lives to move into other roles, moving further westward while constantly fleeing pieces of her past. In it, Mukherjee rejoices in the idea of assimilation and makes it clear that Jasmine needs to travel to America to make something significant of her life, because in the third world she faced only despair and loss.

Jasmine's arranged marriage to a young Indian back in their home town ends abruptly when he is killed in a bombing. Still in her teens but already a widow, Jasmine flees India and, after an odessey, arrives in Florida on a small boat and enters the United States as an illegal immigrant. During her first night in America, which she spends huddled together with some other illegal aliens in a disused motel, she kills the captain of the ship after he has raped her.

Aimlessly walking along a country road not knowing what to do next, Jasmine is picked up by a woman who has helped other illegal immigrants before her. After being given some basic introduction to U.S. society, she sets out to look for a fatherly friend of her dead husband's who is said to be working as a professor. However, when Jasmine actually meets him she realises that he holds some menial job and that for years he has been lying about it in his letters back home.

Disillusioned by this experience, Jasmine wanders on and gets a job as a *nanny*. She falls in love with her employer, and after he and his wife separate, Jasmine has a brief fling with him and soon realises that it is time she moved on. She ends up in a small town in Iowa, where she attracts the attention of an old woman whose son is a rich and influential man as the town's banker, after Jasmine moves in, he is shot and becomes paralysed. Her love in boyfriend, Bud, would like to have a child by her, so she is artificially inseminated. However, near the end of her pregnancy having never married Bud, she decides to leave him again and move to California with her former employer, who has custody of his daughter, Jasmine's former charge.

When Jasmine is suddenly widowed at seventeen, she seems fated to a life of quiet isolation in the small Indian village where she was born. But the force of Jasmine's desires propels her explosively into a larger, more dangerous, and ultimately more life-giving world. In just a few years, Jasmine becomes Jane Ripple Meyer, happily pregnant by a middle-aged Iowa banker and the adoptive mother of a Vietnamese refugee. Jasmine's metamorphosis, with its shocking upheavals and its slow evolutionary steps, illuminates the making of an American mind; but even more powerfully, her story depicts the shifting contours of an America being transformed by her and others like her — our new neighbours friends, and lovers. In Jasmine, Bharati Mukherjee has created a heroine as exotic and unexpected as the many worlds in which she lives.

The protagonist of the novel, Jasmine undergoes several transformations during her journey of life in America, from Jyoti to Jasmine to Jane, and often experiences a deep sense of estrangement resulting in a fluid state of identity. This journey becomes a tale of moral courage, a search for self-awareness and self-assertion. Uprooted from her native land India, Jyoti does her best to introduce herself into the new and alien society as an "immigrant"; the culmination finally indicated in Jasmine's pregnancy with the child of a white man—Bud.

Born in Hasanpur in India, Jyoti has the distinction of being the most beautiful and clever in the family. Her life, like most Indian women, is controlled and dominated by her father and brothers, "Village girls are like cattle, whichever way you lead them, that is the way they will go" (46).

Jyoti, however, seeks a modern and educated husband who keeps no faith in dowries and traditions, and thus finds a US based modern-thinking man, Prakash, who encourages her to study English, and gives a new name, Jasmine. Jasmine gets a new life of freedom and joy. But, ironically enough, this happiness is short-lived as Prakash is killed by a terrorist outfit called the *Khalsa Lions*. In this turn of circumstances, she has to choose between the rigid traditions of her family and perform *Sati*, or continue to live the life of Jasmine in America. Deeply dejected,

Jasmine decides to visit the institute where her husband was supposed to be inducted, and to burn herself a *sati* on its campus. With this view in mind, Jasmine sets off on an agonising trip as an illegal immigrant to Florida, and thus begins her symbolic trip of transformations, displacement, and a search for identity.

Jasmine's first confrontation with the ugliness of the world comes up when the captain of the ship in which she travels takes her to a remote motel of Florida and rapes her remorselessly. But the outraged woman takes her revenge by killing him. After this violent encounter with the cruelties of the world, Jasmine starts afresh, meets Lillian Gordon, the lady who teaches her how to walk and talk like a "true" American. With her help, Jasmine manages to reach New York to earn a living. Among the Punjabi immigrants here, she feels like a helpless widow, terrified of life: "I wanted to distance myself from everything Indian, everything Jyoti-like" (p. 145).

Jasmine is unable to cope with the conservative India represented by the Vadheras and thus spending five months of frustration at Flushing, she sets forth for another adventure to Manhattan to work as a care-giver in the family of Taylor and Wylie Hayes and Duff, their adopted daughter. Taylor gives her a new name "Jase". In a surrounding of human warmth, Jasmine becomes more Americanised, but her instinctive Indian values show up at times. Her essential Indianness does not let her tolerate her the sight of "naked bodies combing their hair in front of dressing mirrors" (p. 171). She feels disgusted with all this: "Truly there was no concept of shame in this society. I'd die before a Sob Sister asked me about Half-face" (p. 171).

She again feels outwitted at Wylie's decision to leave Taylor for the economist Stuart in search of "real" happiness. She comes to realise the liquidity and transitoriness of human relationship in America and is badly disenchanted.

But Jasmine wants to have a balanced view of things and thus loves the positive side of America and appreciates the Americans for their democracy of thought and their work culture. However the restless spirit of Jasmine still forces her to run from New York off to Iowa where she gets shelter by Mother Ripple Mayer who helped her by providing her a job in her son Bud's bank as a teller girl and soon after six months she turns into a live-in companion of Bud who again christens her as "Jane". This development in Jasmine's life indicates her immersion into the liberal American culture as also her transformation from Jasmine into Jane the one who not only enjoys the unmarried company of an American but is also bold enough to carry his child in her womb.

Jasmine sways between the past and the present attempting to come to terms with the two worlds, one of "nativity" and the other as an "immigrant". Hailing from an oppressive and a rural family in India, Jyoti comes to America in search of a more fruitful life and to realise the dreams of her husband. She, thus, begins her journey westward and her quest for a new self. She undergoes her first transformation from a dutiful Hindu wife when she meets the intellectual Taylor who calls her Jase, and then moves on to become Bud's "Jane".

Bharati Mukherjee depicts this transformation and transition as a positive and an optimistic journey. Jasmine creates a new world consisting of new ideas and values, constantly unmasking her past. She tries to establish a new cultural identity by incorporating new desires, skills, and habits. This transition is defined not only in the changes in her attitude, but more significantly in her relationship with men. In India, as Jyoti, she is seen against the backdrop of the rigid and patriarchical Indian society. In America, her self-awareness is reflected in her relationships with Bud, Taylor, and Du. However, her first husband Prakash initiates her transformation from Jyoti to Jane. After her husband's death, Jasmine tries to establish a new cultural identity and in exile, she essays to cultivate "new habits and expressions of life." Thus, caught between the two cultures of the east and west, past and present, old and new, Jasmine constantly "shuttles" in search of a concrete identity. Bharati Mukherjee ends the book on a novel note, and re-emphasises the complex and alternating nature of identity of a woman in exile,

"Then there is nothing I can do. Time will tell if I am a tornado, rubble-maker, arising from nowhere and disappearing into a cloud. I am out the door and in the potholed and rutted driveway, scrambling ahead of Taylor, greedy with wants and reckless from hope" (241).

Jasmine's postcolonial, ethnic characters are post-American, carving out new spaces for themselves from among a constellation of available cultural narratives, never remaining bound by any one, and always fluidly negotiating the boundaries of their past, present, and futures. By subjecting her heroine to multiple codes of society and geographical locales, Bharati Mukherjee seems to send a message that if one has to assimilate oneslf to the mainstream culture of adopted land, one should forget one's past. But for Jasmine the assimilation is not so smooth as it might appear on the surface. All is not well with her in Iowa after Du leaves for Los Angeles to join his sister. His sudden departure shatters Jasmine's world, which she had been nourishing so delicately. Jasmine's alienation and bewilderment becomes explicit in her restless move from one place to another. She often realises her "outsiderness" and "otherness" in America and suffers from an excruciating sense of humiliation and disappointment. Despite all her apparent anguish for Indian culture, she never fully assimilates the American values. In attempting to resolve her crisis of identity through nomenclature and geography from Jyoti to Jasmine, to Jase , and to Jane—and from Hasnaur to Julundhar, to Florida, Manhattan and Iowa, Jasmine fruitlessly tries out all the alternatives. Her external movement has not necessarily meant an internal transformation.

Jasmine is a story of vast uncertainty, resilience, and assimilation. We see the protagonist perpetually facing one obstacle after another as she challenges the idea that her life is destined to become a disaster. She changes into many different characters with each American family that she meets. She is born into a displaced middle class Indian family of nine children as Jyoti, and becomes Jasmine, Jazzy, Jase, and Jane throughout her life. Her multiple identities represent changes in her life and her attempts to assimilate into her new surroundings. Jasmine is caught between many worlds: eastern v. western, Indian v.

American, traditions v. reform, and fate v. control over one's destiny. She embodies the lively and persistent spirit of the hopeful immigrant to America, and her determination to transcend her adversities while embracing the differences in all individuals makes her a very amicable character. The fact that she has gone through all of these names symbolises her intriguing confusion and everlasting desire of finally finding herself.

While many critics and academics have received Mukherjee favourably, she has also faced a good deal of criticism, particularly from East Indian scholars and critics. It has been said that she often represents India in her fiction as a land without hope or a future. She has also been criticised for a tendency to overlook unavoidable barriers of caste, education, gender, race and history in her tales of survivors, particularly within *Jasmine,* giving her characters more opportunities than their social circumstances would realistically allow.

REFERENCES

Edward W. Said. *Reflections On Exile* (Harvard: H U P, 2000)

Bill Ashcroft. Gareth Griffiths and Helen Tiffin, *The Empire Writes Back* (London: Routledge, 1989)

Frederic Jameson. *Post-Modernism or The Cultural Logic of Late Capitalism* (London: Verso, 1991)

All textual quotations from: Mukherjee, Bharati, *Jasmine* (New York: Grove Weidenfield, 1989)

The Inheritance of Class

11

Sarvajit Mukherji

The Inheritance of Loss is a complex, multi-textured novel. Many stories coalesce to craft its rich texture—it can be read as a novel about the experience of the illegal immigrant (Biju's story), the construction of the colonial (Justice Patel's story), the rebellion of the subaltern (Gyan and the GNLF), a bildungsroman (Sai's seeking of maturity) or a novel whose subtext is class consciousness and conflict.

Set in Kalimpong in the turbulent 80s, the background to the novel is one of India's many mutinies, the Gorkhaland agitation which demanded the right to self-determination and a homeland for the Nepali speaking people of India. The main characters of the novel, are all, however, people who have opted to live in Kalimpong, regarding it as either haven or home. For the Afghan princesses and Mrs. Thondup, Kalimpong is a refuge, for Father Booty, Kalimpong is his chosen home, Lola, Noni and Mrs. Sen have quit the fumes and humidity of Kolkata and have moved to the more salubrious climes of Kalimpong to live in retirement, while Uncle Potty is a gentleman farmer from Lucknow.

The motives of Justice J.P. Patel ICS in opting to live in Kalimpong are the most complex. The Judge, the fruit of the British policy of Indianising the Indian Civil Services has withdrawn in anger from the world and settled down in Cho Oyu, a house sold to him by a Scotsman, returning to England. In his efforts to become the proverbial 'brown sahib', Justice Patel has spurned his family, his roots and his culture. He has disowned his parents, his wife and daughter and has opted to live in a part of India where he cannot be identified with his lower middle class, Gujarati beginnings. Cho Oyu may be crumbling and dilapidated, but it still spells colonial class. Justice Patel has bent himself backwards to join the anglicised upper middle class, and because his hold on it is so tenuous, he is supercilious and arrogant, as he is to Sai's tutor Gyan. This group of immigrants from within and without India, form the upper crust of Kalimpong society. They have in common the English tongue and a cosmopolitan, Anglicised culture. They live in the large bungalows built by the British, and their life style is a watered down version of that of the departed Imperial masters. They go to the Gymkhana club in Darjeeling, lunch at the club or at Glenary's, read English novels, have pudding at Christmas, and listen to the BBC. Sai, Justice Patel's grand-daughter, is markedly different from the rest of this closed social group. Sequestered as her life has been, she is open to life's possibilities. By the end of the novel, she is convinced she must leave, or life will pass her by. She is also the only one who has forged links with the underclass—the cook, Gyan and Biju.

In fact, the cook is something of a surrogate father to Sai. When she arrives from a convent in Dehradun, an orphan packed off to her only surviving relation, it is the cook who welcomes her and tries to make her arrival more cheerful by cooking and serving dishes as must please a child. It is the cook who talks to her teacher Noni. He is as affectionate and possessive about her, as he might be about his own child. When the police come to Cho Oyu after the GNLF cadres rob the Judge of his guns and search the cook's quarters, Sai is appalled by how little the cook actually owns. She is humiliated by his humiliation at the hands of the constables. The joy and pride of the cook's life is his son Biju, who he thinks is prospering in America. The fact of the matter is that Biju is an illegal immigrant in the States. As he shifts from kitchen to kitchen making out a miserable existence in the basements of Manhattan, dodging immigration and the police and obsessing about a green card, there is a growing conviction within him that he must return. His life in the basement kitchens of Manhattan is in fact no better than that of the rat that Saeed Saeed catches, viciously kicks and dribbles to death. Out of the exploitation and labour of the illegal migrants of the third world, bloom the wonderous and glittering restaurants—variously decorated with mirrors, blow ups of Marilyn Monroe or Gandhi—for which Biju works. The cook, blissfully oblivious of Biju's plight continues to boast about his son and send him names of more hopefuls, sons of his friends, lining up for migration to the USA. Lola and Noni are rather wary of Sai's affection for cook.

The distinction between the classes, they feel, must be maintained by keeping a distance. Personal conversations with servants must not be encouraged lest something too personal emerge like the passion of Kesang, their cook, for the milkman.

The novel opens with the underclass beginning to assert itself—an assertion that leads to unprecedented violence, loss of life and property and damage to the economy and infrastructure of Kalimpong. Among the peaks and slopes of the hills, along the reinforcements to the dizzying road climbing up beside the gushing Teesta, between the monasteries and prayer flags appear menacing slogans, kukhri wielding boys rallying on the roads roar them out, there are more bandh days than ordinary days and tea garden managers are kidnapped and held to ransom. Suddenly, everyone is talking of insurgency.

The simmering discontent in the hills first impinges on the life of Justice Patel's household when the GNLF guerillas force their entry into Cho Oyu and leave only after they have stolen guns and victuals, and humiliated Justice Patel by forcing him to serve them tea. In a burst of activity, the police arrest a local drunk, charge him with stealing the guns, torture and blind him. This is the first of a spate of torture and victimisation that further fans the fire in the mountain. When not drunk, this victim of police brutality used to work as a labourer repairing the roads regularly damaged by rain and landslides. His helpless wife and father show up at the gates of Cho Oyu, seeking justice and help. But the judge has his own perception of the situation. 'Give these people a bit and one could find oneself supporting the whole family forever after, a constantly multiplying family, no doubt, because they might have no food, the husband might be blind and with broken legs, and the woman might be anaemic and bent, but they'd still pop out an infant every nine months. If you let such people get an inch, they'd take everything you had —' (264).

In desperation they turn to Sai , but she too turns away. She has been betrayed by Gyan, he has spurned her love and rejected her proffered reconciliation. Most of all he has betrayed her class. It is he who has informed the GNLF cadres about the guns. He is part of the movement that is aimed at people like Sai, her friends and family. And Gyan is definitely lowest of low middle class, struggling towards gentility as Sai realises when she sees where he lives

'There were houses like this everywhere, of course, common to those who had just struggled to the far edge of the middle class—just to the edge, only just, holding on desperately—but were at every moment being undone...' (256).

In comparison, Cho Oyu represents class.

'Cho Oyu might be crumbling, but it once had been majestic; it had its past if not its future, and that might be enough—(257).

The victims retaliate by stealing Mutt, the Judge's Irish setter. Inadvertently, they have struck where it hurts Justice Patel the most. If there is one creature on earth that Justice Patel loves, it is his dog Mutt. Justice Patel has spent years with his cook, but he has neither regard nor sympathy for him. Sai is his only surviving relative, but he has no affection for her; his repressed, self-conscious and arrogant nature finds an outlet in expressing affection for Mutt, who adores him. Originally, Justice Patel belonged to a race and class that has no use for dogs. But years ago, as an ICS aspirant studying in England, when he never spoke to a single soul, if he could help it, his only companion was his landlady's dog. In England, where he learnt to despise his colour, background, race and nation, Justice Patel learnt to love and care for animals. In fact, pets are also an indication of class in the novel. Lola and Noni have their cat Mustapha. He is part of the dream Lola and Joydeep had—mists, sweet peas, books and cat—a dream of retirement in a cottage in Kalimpong. Father Booty has his cows and his dream of a Swiss-style economy for Kalimpong. When Mutt is stolen, everyone has a horror story to relate about stolen pets: Uncle Potty's Kutta Sahib was stolen, the Afghan princesses' Afghan hounds were stolen and eaten. Gyan and his family living in the slum of Bong Basti, have their chickens. When Sai, having waited in vain for Gyan to appear at Cho Oyu, sets out in search of him and arrives at Bong Basti, the first thing that strikes her are the chickens.

"Chickens, chickens, chicken bought to supplement a tiny income. The birds had never revealed themselves to her so clearly; a grotesque bunch, rape and violence being enacted, hens being hammered and pecked as they screamed and flapped, attempting escape from the rapist rooster" (256).

That Mutt enjoys a higher status in Justice Patel's world than most human beings is amply clear. When the two destitute Lepchas appear at his gate, Justice Patel has no help to offer. He won't even talk to the authorities suggesting that they might have made a mistake and arrested the wrong man. But he leaves no stone unturned in his search for Mutt. He visits officials and is ridiculed for his efforts, he speaks to persons he has never spoken to before. He even defies the curfew and raises dire suspicions in the mind of the soldier on patrol duty, but he continues his search. The climax comes when he thrashes the cook with his slipper for being negligent in his care of Mutt. The cook's fate is identical to that of Mutt now. Her new owners keep her tied to a tree and kick her for no reason. This is also a moment of truth for Sai, who realises that she must get away, if she can.

Sai is aghast at the attitudes she has unconsciously imbibed when she attacks Gyan for having betrayed her and her world. Initially attracted to Sai by the chemistry of sex, Gyan is awed by her class and sophistication—Sai, in her scarlet kimono, gilded with dragons, is a 'splendid' being, far removed from anything that he had known before. But as Gyan becomes aware of his identity as a deprived Gorkha youth courtesy the GNLF, these very qualities of Sai become the wedge that drives them apart. Characteristically, their first fight is about a Christmas party at Mon Ami. Gyan's resentment of the class Sai belongs to, his ambivalent attitude towards her, leads him to inform the GNLF about the guns in Cho Oyu.

'The chink she had provided into another world gave him just enough room to kick; he could work against her, define the conflict in his life that he felt all along, but in a cotton wooly way. In pushing her away, an energy was born, a purpose whittled'(260).

Sai realises all this when she sees the shanty in Bong Basti, where Gyan lives. She realises that she just represents her class to Gyan.

"You hate me... for big reasons, that have nothing to do with me. You are n't being fair"(p.257).

But having realised that now only her class identifies her to Gyan, she retaliates by attacking his class.

Low class family, uncultured, arranged marriage types...' and 'typical of you people, demand and take and then spit on what you have been given' (261). And as he flings her into the lantana bush and thrashes her with a stick, the relationship is irrevocably broken..

The victims are on both sides of the class divide. The most poignant case is that of Nimmi, Justice Patel's wife. Married at fourteen to the brightest boy in the community on his way to England, Jemubhai Popatlal Patel, Nimmi is a victim from the first. She is married for her dowry that enables Jemubhai to travel to England to further his quest for the ICS. He returns a different man — a Westernised Oriental Gentleman, an ICS, who is part of the ruling elite. He now wants to metamorphose his wife into a Westernised Oriental Lady. When, despite the ministrations of Miss Enid Potts, her governess, Nimmi remains stubbornly Indian, her husband turns savage. Nimmi is beaten, starved, raped, humiliated and finally packed off to her paternal home, where she gives birth to her daughter, Sai's mother. Nimmi's tragedy continues. Her Uncle, now the *pater familias* after her father's death, turns her out because her husband will not take her back and Nimmi lives a life of destitution and deprivation at her sister's home till her death by burning.

Lola is another victim of the great class divide. When Nepalese squatters forcibly occupy the vegetable garden in Mon Ami, begin cutting down the fruit trees and building huts, Lola petitions Pradhan, the GNLF chief in Kalimpong for relief and help. Old and widowed as she is, she is insulted, humiliated and sexually taunted by the 'King of Kalimpong'. On her return to Mon Ami, Lola locks herself in the bathroom and curses her husband for having opted to live in a part of the country to which they do not belong. If Biju is an exile in the USA, Lola, Noni and Uncle Potty are exiles in their own country and are perpetual outsiders, vulnerable targets for local agitations who can be displaced and destroyed at any time. As the country gets further and further sub-divided, it is people like Lola, Noni, Uncle Potty and Father Booty who are the victims. They are not accepted in their own country. For the GNLF, they are foreigners stealing the timber and exporting the tea. Lola is sure that she has identified the genesis of the problem:

'This state-making' Lola continued, 'biggest mistake that fool Nehru made. Under his rules any group of idiots can stand up demanding a new state and get it too...' (128).

Lola has sensed how class conflict compounds the problem.

'It did'nt come from nothing, even Lola knew, but from an old feeling of anger that could'nt be divorced from Kalimpong. It was part of every breath....

These people could name them, recognize them—the few rich—but Lola and Noni could barely distinguish between the individuals making up the crowd of the poor.

It did matter, buying tinned ham roll in a rice and dal country; it did matter to live in a big house and sit beside a heater in the evening, even one that sparked and shocked; it did matter to fly to London and return with chocolates filled with kirsch; it did matter that others could not' (241).

The Gorkhaland agitation erupts. Nehruvian socialism has ensured class distinctions of the kind seen in Kalimpong. It has ensured that majority of the population remain poor and deprived and backwardness become a virtue. Gyan feels he is rejected in interviews because of persons who belong to Sai's class. Young people of Sai's class like Lola's Pixie and Mrs. Sen's Munmun have all fled to the West. Also looking Westward are young people of the underclass like Biju. The labour of these young people fuel the progress of the First World.

By the end of the novel, the two narratives coalesce. Biju is back in Kalimpong. He is at peace now for he no longer feels an alien and is no longer on the run. Yet this homecoming is also flawed. Robbed by the GNLF cadres, he is as destitute as he was when he left—his years of tribulation in America and all his father's dreams of wealth all have been in vain. Sai, on the other hand, is ready to leave Kalimpong. She is no longer seeking her own happiness. 'Never again could she think there was but one narrative and that this narrative belonged only to herself, that she might create her own tiny happiness and live safely within it'(323) She is willing to merge her story with the myriad other stories, but for that to happen, she must leave. She must go somewhere, where life will not pass her by. And then she sees Biju, the returned native, toiling up the slope in his absurd nightgown. The two journeys, one towards 'home' and the other away from 'home' are two semi-circular narratives that coalesce to form the whole that is *The Inheritance of Loss*.

BIBLIOGRAPHY

1. Kiran Desai. *The Inheritance of Loss*, Viking, New Delhi 2006.
2. Williams Raymond. *Marxism and Literature*, OUP, New York, 1973.

Ice-Candy Man: A Postcolonial Study

12

R.P. Pradhan

A postcolonial reading of Bapsi Sidhwa's *Ice-Candy Man* seems to be relevant in spite of its several other aspects. The novel is set in the transitional period of India's partition in 1947. The novelist calls in question the history of partition written by the British and the Indian writers. As a postcolonial writer, she makes an attempt to write an alternate history to counter the Indian and the British points of views. Her outlook is anti-colonial and as such she writes in the spirit of a Pakistani national. Her Parsi-Zoroastrian background is also expressive from time to time. Being a Parsi woman, she introduces an eight year old Parsi girl as the narrator of the novel. She feels identical with the handicapped girl as she herself was afflicted with polio at an early age. She speaks through the consciousness of the girl who happens to be a deficient and under-privileged member of society. In that way, she voices the anxiety of the suffering and the suppressed people during the period.

The novelist shows that in the seething atmosphere of partition, the composite culture of India which had been coming from the past was disappearing by and by and different communities had become conscious of their individual status. The Parsis also aspired for the creation of their cultural autonomy. Lenny saw how men under religious fervour got organised in several groups and discussed the problem of partition that appeared to be imminent. The reactions of Lenny in the troubled atmosphere reflected her Parsi attitudes. In her opinion, the small minority community felt reduced to "irrelevant nomenclatures."[1] The communal turmoil made the Parsis aware of the religious differences. They became conscious of having their separate identity. Their feelings find expression in this way:

> Gandhi, Jinnah, Nehru, Iqbal, Tara Singh, Mountbatten are names I hear. And I become aware of religious differences. It is sudden. One day everybody is themselves—and the next day they are Hindu, Muslim, Sikh, Christian. People shrink, dwindling into symbols. Ayah is no longer just my all-encompassing Ayah—she is also a token. A Hindu.[2]

The novelist reveals that in the traditional history, the Parsis are ignored and it is assumed that they did not play a role in the historical process of partition. She contradicts such opinions and shows that Parsi community was not a passive spectator of the communal scene. It played silent but active role in rendering services to the suffering people. Lenny's parents and her aunt Godmother helped the victims of partition. They helped the orphaned Ranna and the suffering woman Hamida. The Godmother Rodabai went out of her way to rescue Ayah (real name Shanta) in returning to her relatives in Lahore. Ayah had been abducted by the mob which was related to Ice-Candy-Man. She had been kept in a brothel of Hira Mandi. The Ice-Candy-Man forcibly married Ayah and changed her name to Mumtaz. He recited poems of love to her but even love appeared to be powerless before communal frenzy. Ayah revolted against her newly acquired Muslim identity. With the help of Lenny's Godmother, she was taken to recovered woman's camp and was sent back to her family in Amritsar. The Ice-Candy-Man followed her there in vain. Their relation was broken forever and love did not conquer communal hatred.

The Godmother was fearless enough to call Ice-Candy Man a "shameless badmash! Nimakharam! Faithless!" (248) a "low-born, two-bit evil little mouse" (248) and the "son of pigs and pimps" (249). The Ice-candy-Man surrendered to Godmother. The Godmother infused life and spirit among the suffering people like Ayah. She consoled Ayah in these words:

> That was fated daughter. It can't be undone. But it can be forgiven...Worse things are forgiven. Life goes on and the business of living buries the debris of our pasts. Hurt, happiness...all fade impartially... to make way for fresh joy and new sorrow. That's the way of life.[3]

The novelist shows that such acts of kindness and understanding performed by the Parsis during the days of partition cannot be ignored and they point to the humanitarian outlook of the Parsis. They played vital role in rendering services to the sufferers.

The novel is set in pre-partition India in Lahore. It belongs to the genre of partition novel. While other novels like *A Bend In the Ganges* (1964), *Azadi* (1975), *Train To Pakistan (1956)* and *The Dark Dancer (1959)* present the Indian views on partition, *Ice-Candy Man* brings before us the Pakistani version of events. Bapsi Sidhwa's attitude is reflected in this context:

> The main motivation grew out of my reading of a good deal of literature on the Partition of India and Pakistan........ What has been written has been written by the British and the Indians. Naturally, they reflect their bias. And they have, I felt after I'd researched the book, been unfair to the Pakistanis. As a writer, as a human being, one just does not tolerate injustice. I felt whatever little I could do to correct an injustice I would like to do. I have just let facts speak for themselves, and through my research I found out what the facts were.[4]

The title of the novel is symbolic of the character of the politicians of partition. When the novel appeared in 1988 in London, its original title was *Ice-Candy Man*. In the 1991 American edition it was changed to "Cracking India." It was thought that the expression "Ice-Candy" would be confused with drugs by the Americans. However, its original title *Ice-Candy Man* is more communicating. The title bears political connotations. The word "icy" points to unstable quality of the politicians who were engaged in determining the fate of the nation. In their outlook, they appeared to be icy and slippery. They were not firm and consistent in their political views. They did not maintain a stable character. They changed their decision from time to time. They were just like the ice-candy-man who changed his roles in a frequent manner. When there was fall in the sale of ice-candy in the cold weather, he changed his profession and became a birdman who took pride in deceiving his customers. When there was increasing communal trouble, he became "allah's telephone"(107) and gave an impression that he was in direct line of communication with God. He posed as a holy man but really he was unholy and acted like a pretender. Towards the end of the novel, the ice-candy man took up the profession of pimping. In that way, his work was deceptive and immoral. He made use of his sharp tongue and rhetorical speeches in throwing dust in the eyes of the people. In view of the novelist, several politicians were indulging in such kinds of role.

The word "ice" bears another meaning also. According to Sidhwa, the politicians during the days of partition were as cold as ice to the sufferings of the people. The battle for partition had caused violence and bloodshed but the politicians remained indifferent to the terrible loss of human life. The novelist includes the name of Gandhi, Nehru, Subhash Chandra Bose and the English Viceroy Lord Louis Mountbatten in this matter.

As a postcolonial writer, Sidhwa regards partition as much a part of Pakistani history as it a part of Indian history. In this context, some of her views regarding it appear to be enlightened but some of them are full of personal prejudices. She shows an independent Parsi attitude when she does not endorse the two nation theory propounded by Jinnah behind the creation of Pakistan. Again, in her opinion, the great communal divide was not inevitable as some writers have been thinking, it was an outcome of growing communal frenzy which had been created by the circumstances. The ice-candy-man supports this view when he says that the religious and cultural differences are created by men in a false manner and they are also fostered deliberately. The novelist holds the view that the religious differences were exploited on the eve of partition. Indirectly, she seems to think that the communal feeling was not an offshoot of partition, its flame had already been fanned by the then politicians. In her view, the feeling of bigotry shall go on spreading if people do not learn lessons from history. In this way, Sidhwa expresses a broad outlook towards the theme of partition.

However, in matters of the presentation of the great political figures of the time, she does not appear to do justice.

Her attitude towards Mahatma Gandhi, J.L. Nehru, Lord Mountbatten and Subhash Chandra Bose is not favourable. These figures are either caricatured or they are presented in unfavourable manner. Sidhwa appears in the novel like an iconoclast when she tarnishes the sublime image of Mahatma Gandhi. The Indian and the British writers have always held Gandhi in high esteem. Lenny does not like Gandhi and thinks of him as "an improbable mixture of a demon and a clown" (87). In the novel, Gandhi makes a visit to Lahore. His visit to this city is not historically accurate but it is a matter of fictional description on the basis of his visit to several other places in India. Gandhi is shown talking to Lenny and her mother. The child Lenny is very much confused because she cannot understand how this small and frail looking man can become so popular in India and in the world. She discovers a feeling of pity and tolerance in the eyes of Mahatma Gandhi: "everything that is feminine, funny, gentle, loving" (87). The reaction of Lenny about Gandhi is

> He is a Man who loves women. And lame children. And the untouchable sweeper's constipated girl-child best.[5]

Lenny's reactions towards Gandhi is very much mixed. She says:

> He (Gandhi) is small, dark, shriveled, old. He looks just like Hari, our gardener, except he has a disgruntled, disgusted and irritable look, and no one'd dare pull off his dhoti! He wears only the loin cloth and his black and thin torso is naked.[6]

Gandhi's visit to Lahore becomes a matter of parody and fun for the novelist. Gandhi is not considered to be a political saint as he is regarded by the Indian writers. Lenny's comparison of Gandhi with her gardener is nothing sort of mockery and it cannot be approved even in the case of a child like Lenny.

Sidhwa also expresses her reaction to the Gandhi film which presents him as a saint. She makes a comment that Gandhi is not human in that film and Sidhwa has tried to humanise him in her novel.

Sidhwa is further critical of the role of Gandhi. She expresses her national bias when she says that the partition favoured India over Pakistan:

> The Hindus are being favoured over the Muslims by the remnants of the Raj. Now that its objective to divide India is achieved, the British favour Nehru over Jinnah. Nehru is Kashmiri, they grant him Kashmir. Spurning logic, defying rationale, ignoring the consequence of bequeathing a Muslim state to the Hindus.............They grant Nehru Gurdaspur and Pathankot without which Muslim Kashmir cannot be secured.[7]

The most destructive and unjust comment which a novelist like Sidhwa can make is regarding the political honesty of Mahatma Gandhi. Sidhwa says:

> Gandhi really sowed the seeds of Partition and turned the whole independence struggle into a Hindu movement. It's hard for people in the West, where he is deified, to regard him as a petty manipulative politician.[8]

Such comments are not sane and they are the product of a mind which is full of political prejudices. Laurel Graeber also remarks, "Bapsi Sidhwa has attempted to give a Pakistani perspective to the Partition of India."[9]

There is another disparaging remark about Gandhi which is not less insulting. It seems to be made by a mature narrator:

> It wasn't until some years later—when I realized the full scope and dimension of the massacres—that I comprehended the concealed nature of the ice lurking deep beneath the hypnotic and dynamic femininity of Gandhi's non-violent exterior.[10]

As a postcolonial writer, Bapsi Sidhwa has got every right to make a reassessment of the personalities of the political leaders of partition but she does not appear to be just when she indulges in the act of character assassination of a great figure like Gandhi. Contrary to her view, Gandhi is always the same man inside and outside. For him, non-violence is not an external show but an integral part of his spiritual life. Truth and non-violence are the fundamental ethics of Gandhi and his spiritual agony for the suffering people is unlimited and it cannot be given the image of crocodile tears.

In contrast to Gandhi, the image of Jinnah has been exalted. Sidhwa expresses in a very strong manner that the description of Jinnah in the history of the Indian and the British writers is not given in a fair and just manner. In her opinion, Jinnah has been caricatured "as a very stiff villain of the piece." She tells David Montenegro:

> And I felt in *Ice-Candy Man*, I was just redressing, in a small way, a very grievous wrong that has been done to Jinnah and Pakistanis by many Indian and British writers. They've dehumanized him, made him a symbol of the sort of person who brought about the Partition of India........ Whereas in reality he was the only constitutional man who didn't sway crowds by rhetoric.[11]

In order to contradict the British and Indian versions of partition, the novelist elevates the image of Jinnah and presents him as an "ambassador of Hindu-Muslim unity" (160). In this respect, she refers to the statement of Sarojini Naidu, the Indian poetess:

> The calm hauteur of his accustomed reserve masks, for those who knew him, a naive and eager humanity, an intuition quick and tender as a woman's, a humour gay and winning as a child's—pre-eminently rational and practical, discreet and dispassionate in his estimate and acceptance of life, the obvious sanity and serenity of his worldly wisdom effectually disguise a shy and splendid idealism which is of the very essence of the man.[12]

The passage brings into light the "sanity and serenity" of the practical wisdom of Jinnah. It raises the stature of his personality to a great extent. The novelist regrets how "ambassador of Hindu-Muslim Unity" has been misrepresented in films of Gandhi and also in the books of the British and Indian writers. She writes:

> Today forty years later, in films of Gandhi's and Mountbatten's times, in books by British and Indian scholars, Jinnah who for a decade was known as an "ambassador of Hindu-Muslim Unity", is caricatured and portrayed as a monster.[13]

In drawing the portrait of Jinnah, Bapsi Sidhwa performs the function of a postcolonial writer. She tries to justify the faith of her people in their art, religion, history and political sagacity of the leaders. She counters the colonial version by giving an alternate conception of history. She undercuts not only the British but also the Indian version of history.

There is reference to the Parsi wife of Jinnah. She was an extremely beautiful woman. She had married Jinnah against the wishes of her wealthy father and other members of the family. It is reported that their marriage was not very happy and she died broken-hearted. The novelist stands in favour of Jinnah and says that Jinnah also died of a broken heart. Every statement of Bapsi Sidhwa is favourable in respect of Jinnah.

The novelist makes an assessment of Nehru's personality in her own way. According to her, Nehru has been a shrewd politician who "will walk off with the lion's share" (131) in spite of all the effort made by Jinnah. The ice-candy-man points out that Nehru is "a sly one...He's got Moutbatten eating out of his one hand and the English's wife out of his other what not... He's the one to watch" (131).

Sidhwa in her novel describes the cruelties done by the Hindu, Mulsim and the Sikhs. However, she makes one particular concession regarding the Muslims. She expresses in a very clear manner that her sympathies go with the muslim victims. She describes the attack of the muslim village of Pir Pindo and shows how men, women and children are killed by the Sikhs. The villagers are further warned against an impending Akali attack. Individual acts of relief are there but they can help only a few victims, and cannot reduce the sufferings caused by organised violence.

As a postcolonial writer, Bapsi Sidhwa is very particular about her use of English. She faces the question whether she should write in a traditional language which has been inherited from the colonial power or whether she should use her own English. It is admitted that the imperialists make use of their language to control the mind and the spirit of the colonised people. In such condition, there is a great danger of being colonised on the cultural level if the native do not become conscious of their use of language. Bapsi Sidhwa makes an alteration in the traditional English to suit her interest. Her original language is Gujrati, her second language is Urdu and her third language is English. She admits that it is not a bad thing to write in English because it is a rich language. However, her use of English is somewhat different. She uses several Gujrati and Urdu words in her English expression. In that way, she makes it native and original. Sidhwa's English may be called new English because it is mixed with words from native language. She states in her interview with Feroza Jussawalla:

> My first language of speech is Gujrati, my second is Urdu, my third is English. But as far as reading and writing goes I can read and write best in English. I'm a tail-end product of the Raj. This is the case with a lot of people in India and Pakistan. They're condemned to write in English, but I don't think this is such a bad thing because English is a rich language. Naturally it is not my first language. I'm more at ease talking in Gujrati and Urdu. After moving to America, I realized that all my sentences in English were punctuated with Gujrati and Urdu words.[14]

Some of her native words have been translated and some few words have been left in their original form. Translation of individual native words cannot convey the original meaning all the time. For example the word "Kotha" (267) is translated in the novel as "roof (267) but its traditional meaning in the native language is the place of prostitution. There is gap between the word "Kotha" and "roof" in respect of meaning. "Kotha" becomes a cultural sign. Again, some native words have not been translated such as "Sarkar" (157), "Yaar" (91), "Doolha" (180), "Chachi" (199), "haramzadi" (45), etc. The untranslated words refer to the postcolonial spirit of the writer who wants to express the cultural differences between the colonisers and the colonised. Again, the novelist quotes several urdu poets in her description to bring into light the importance of Muslim culture. The lines from Iqbal's poetry refer to the anti-colonial spirit of the novelist:

> The times have changed; the world has changed its mind.
> The European's mystery is erased.
> The secret of his conjuring tricks is known;
> The Frankish wizard stands and looks amazed.

Iqbal brushes aside the notion that the white race is superior to all other races. Sidhwa through these lines also expresses her idea that the British claim of civilising the black people of Asia and Africa is baseless. Their "conjuring tricks" is exposed and is known to all the people. The colonisers like the British are blamed for introducing a few diseases in India. Colonel Bharucha says:

> If anyone's to blame, blame the British ! There was no polio in India till they brought it here![16]

Lenny's father also refers to the same thing:

> There was no syphilis in India until the British Came.[17]

Thus, *Ice-Candy Man* calls in question the British and the Indian versions of History and provides an alternative history which is governed by native point of view. It also expresses autobiographical feelings of the novelist who asserts her point of view that the Parsi community during the political agitation of Partition was not marginalised as it is given by some orthodox historians but played an active and silent role. Again, the novelist's use of native English is expressive of her postcolonial literature. The ultimate motto of the novelist finds expression in this way:

> I think a lot of readers in Pakistan, especially with *Ice-Candy Man*, feel that I've given them a voice, which they did not have before. They have always been portrayed in a very unfavourable light. It's been fashionable to kick Pakistan, and it's been done again and again by various writers living in the West.......... And I feel, if there's one little thing one could do, it's to make people realize: we are not worthless because We inhabit a poor country that is seen by Western eyes as a primitive, fundamentalist country only.[18]

REFERENCES

1. Sidhwa, Bapsi. *Ice-Candy Man*, New Delhi, Penguin: 1989. p. 94.
2. *Ibid.*, 93.
3. *Ibid.*, 262.
4. *Ibid.*, 36.
5. *Ibid.*, 87.

6. *Ibid.*, 86.
7. *Ibid.*, 159.
8. *Ibid.*, 11.
9. Graeber, Laurel. "The seeds of Partition" *New York Times*, Oct. 6, 1991, p. 110.
10. Sidhwa, Bapsi. *Ice-Candy Man*, New Delhi, Penguin: 1989, p. 88.
11. Montenegro, David. *Points of Departure-International Writers on writing and Politics*, 1989, p. 50.
12. Sidhwa, Bapsi. *Ice-Candy Man*, New Delhi, Penguin: 1989. p. 161
13. *Ibid.*, 160.
14. Jussawalla, Feroza and Reed Way Dasenbrock. Ed. *Interviews with Writers of the Post-Colonial World*, 1990. p. 214.
15. Sidhwa, Bapsi. *Ice-Candy Man*, New Delhi, Penguin: 1989. p. 111.
16. *Ibid.*, 16
17. *Ibid.*, 61
18. Montenegro, David. *Point of Departure-International Writers on writing and Politics*, 1989, p. 51.

Jhumpa Lahiri: Influential Women Characters

13

Susmita Bhattacharya

The most significant insights of contemporary America can be glimpsed in the works of immigrant writers—Jhumpa Lahiri (*Interpreter of Maladies*, *The Namesake*), or Irish Immigrant author Frank Mc Court in *Tis* or British born Bangladeshi Monica Ali in *Bricklane* or Bharati Mukherjee in her novel *Jasmine*. Jhumpa Lahiri emerged as an eagerly watched literary star with her short-story collection *Interpreter of Maladies* which won her the Pulitzer Prize for fiction 2000. This London-born writer of Bengali origin became the first Asian to win this prestigious American prize which over the decades had gone to such quintessentially American novelists, as Ernest Hemingway, William Faulkner and Noriman Mailer.

Lahiri's superb craftsmanship and literary talents enfold in this collection and serve her well in her debut novel *The Namesake* which continues this theme of navigating between cultures and the immigrant identity. Her stories, except for a few, present the immigrant experience through the women characters.

An immigrant woman's position, is unique, privileged and powerful. Like the great epics, Odyssey and Ramayana, her story is also that of a traveler. She journeys to the promised land and battles adversity, both mental and material. What distinguishes a woman immigrant is her sensitivity, her depth of involvement with the "host" country into which she, in whatever spirit enters. This intensity of engagement differentiates her from a traveler, a tourist, a slave transported across an ocean, or even an exile. It empowers such a character to bring scrutiny to the deepest acknowledged and unacknowledged beliefs and practices of the "host" country even as it captures the immigrant woman's striving for relocation in an alien country. Race and racism are special concerns—the non-white immigrants in a pre-dominantly white society. Other important concerns include nostalgia as well as guilt for the "home country" and intergenerational conflicts between immigrant parents and American born children. They deal with the self and spirit viewed through the safety of the prosperous western prism. Sonia with Gogol in *The Namesake* dread their holidays to Kolkata, the crowds and the discomfort, and rejoice in their return, "once again free to quarrel. To sleep for as long as they like."[1] For all the trouble these characters endure, their dauntless participation in the Great American Dream is what ultimately liberates them.

Lahiri's art is both prolific and powerful in that it conveys a genuine experience. She admits working "very hard" for it: "There are other things that I think of as pleasures in my life, like eating a good meal, being with someone I love, or seeing a beautiful piece of art. Writing is work — writing is a vital part of my existence and the way I think about and experience life. It is all very connected to my well-being as a person."[2] Writing grounded her, entranced her and was also an escape. Growing up brown and "foreign" in a town where white was the predominant theme had its challenges. There was the persistent feeling of other, nor American enough, not Indian enough, of constantly straddling fences, stretching identities. The complications of being a hyphenated American—Indian American - London-born Deshi inform her work. She was born in London of Bengali parents, her father a librarian and mother, a teacher. She grew up in Rhode Island, U.S., and has visited her parents' home city of Kolkata several times. Every visit was an emotional, see-saw across continents and cultures. As her central character of the last story, "The Third and Final Continent' whose transplantation is successful very aptly sums up the experience of life long transcultural voyage—still, there are times I am bewildered by each mile I have travelled, each meal I have eaten, each person I have known, each room in which I have slept."[3] Though the sphere of her work is very much the sphere of her own life—New England and New York, with Kolkata always hovering in the background it is America which emerges as a real presence. The characters must struggle and come to terms with what it means to live here, to be brought up here, to belong and not belong here. For these culturally displaced characters, the question of identity is as particularly vexing as for Lahiri. She has "never known how to answer the question" "where are you from?" If I say I am from Rhode Island, people are seldom satisfied. They want to know more, based on such things as my name, my appearance, etc. Alternatively, if I say I am from India, a place where I was not born and have never lived, this is also inaccurate." Lahiri has wonderfully transmuted her felt-experience in her art.

Maladies is a rich mosaic of women immigrants at different stages of their adaptation to the American life, with all its triumphs and failures. The exotic trappings of these stories, sketched on a canvas that stretches backwards in time and space, give them the universal appeal of a traveller's tale. The accounts have a multi-cultural richness. The description of food, clothes and festivals is in a deft language. Lahiri believes "Food is a very deep part of people's lives and it has incredible meaning beyond the obvious nutritional aspects. My parents have given up so many basic things coming here from the life they once knew—family, love, connections—and food is one thing they've really held on to."[5] Mrs. Sen's presents with great subtlety and sympathy the nostalgia an immigrant woman feels for India. Her alienness on American soil is vividly articulated— "Here, in this place where Mr. Sen has brought me, I cannot sometimes sleep in so much silence."[6] Lahiri skillfully employs the boy Eliot's perspective to portray Mrs. Sen's adjustment problem. Eliot enjoys her chip vegetables seated on newspapers on the living room floor. "Instead of a knife she used a blade that is curved like the prow of a Viking ship sailing to battle in distant seas."[7] To the boy Mrs. Sen is as exotic as the blue aerogram she receives from her home "crammed with stamps showing a bald man at a spinning wheel, and blackened by postmarks."[8] Mrs. Sen, who's trying hard to learn driving, explains to Eliot's mother that at home they have a chauffer.

When Eliot's mother questions "—in India?" Mrs. Sen's reply evokes strong sentiments "Yes, every thing is there."[9] Eliot soon understands that "when Mrs. Sen said home, she meant India, not the apartment where she sat chopping vegetables." And that there are two things which delight her, letters from home and whale fish from the seaside.

The cultural transition of the Bengalis is presented with a subtle touch in the story after which the collection is named. A travelling Bengali American couple hire a Gujarati tour guide Mr. Kapasi, domiciled in Orissa. Mr. Kapasi is smitten by desire for Mrs. Das but is shocked to discover how little she cared for relations, including with casual acquaintances and her husband and children. Here is described the plight of "a woman not yet thirty, who loved neither her husband nor her children, who had already fallen out of love with life."[11] Her confession depresses him:— "I have terrible urges, Mr. Kapasi, to throw things away. One day I had the urge to throw everything I own out of the window, the television, the children, every thing .... "[12]. Her alienation is pathetic, there being no close friends to whom she can reach out; "There was no one to confide in about him at the end of a difficult day, or to share a passing thought or a worry. Her parents now lived on the other side of the world, but she had never been very close to them, anyway. After marrying so young she was overwhelmed by it all, having a child so quickly, and nursing and warming up bottles of milk and testing their temperature against her wrist ...."[13].

Lahiri's technique helps her get at the inner weave of her characters. In 'A Temporary Matter', a young couple who have fallen out-of-love are playing a bitter-sweet game trying to cope up with their loss. Shobha and Shukumar had not eaten together for months. Now, in the dark, with no lights, they are somehow able to talk to each other again, exchange confessions and come closer.

Her novel *The Namesake* is told from several points of view, Ashima's view point is relevant. The Bengali bride who weds Ashoke in an arranged marriage and moves with him to Cambridge, Mass.; "For being a foreigner, Ashima is beginning to realise is a sort of lifelong pregnancy .... a perpetual wait, a constant burden, a continuous feeling out of sorts. It is an ongoing responsibility, a paranthesis in what had been ordinary life, only to discover that that previous life had vanished, replaced by something more complicated and demanding, like pregnancy, being a foreigner, Ashima believes is something that elicits the same curiosity from strangers, the same combination of pity and respect."[14]

Lahiri's exceptional power of observation has shaped these intimate and incisive portraits of her women immigrants. She has succeeded in displaying through them human conditions that have universal resonance. Lahiri herself refutes that she's "representing a group. I would never claim to be doing that. These characters are a very few examples of the range of experience out there. I find it gratifying just to work with words, with language, to work through memories, experiences, observations, imagined things and situations, all of that combined, to try to make things come to life on the page."[15] And these life-like women immigrants unravel, as only a feminist perspective can, many previously overlooked aspects of contemporary American life.

NOTES

1. *The Namesake.*
2. Interview by Alden Mudge, 2/21/2005.
3. *Interpreter of Maladies*, Harper. Collins, New Delhi, 2000, p. 198.
4. Interview.
5. Interview.
6. *Interpreter of Maladies*, p. 115.
7. *Ibid.*, 114.
8. *Ibid.*, 121.
9. *Ibid.*, 113.
10. *Ibid.*, 116.
11. *Ibid.*, 66.
12. *Ibid.*, 65.
13. *Ibid.*, 63.
14. *The Namesake.*
15. Interview to Alden Mudge, Sept. 2003.

Jhumpa Lahiri: An Articulate Commentator of the Maladies of Indian Immigrants

14

Supriya Shukla

When two cultures cast their shadows on a personality, the penumbra of creativity often brings forth a brilliance which attains global relevance. Jhumpa Lahiri's Bengali lineage, her birth in the United Kingdom and her life at Boston in the United States has armed her with multiple paradigms of thinking, something that is well reflected in her writings.

Jhumpa Lahiri's *Interpreter of Maladies* a collection of nine distinct stories, addresses sensitive dilemmas in the lives of Indians or Indian immigrants. Maladies accurately diagnosed and misinterpreted, matters both temporary and life changing, relationships in flux and unshakeable, unexpected blessings and sudden calamities, and the power of survival — these are among the themes of Jhumpa Lahiri's extraordinary, Pulitzer-Prize winning debut collection of stories, *Interpreter of Maladies.* The majority of the stories are set in the North Eastern United States, but some are set in India. Whether set in Boston or Bengal, these sensitive stories spiced with humour and subtle detail, speak with universal eloquence to anyone who has ever felt the yearnings of exile or the emotional confusion of the outsider. Travelling from India to New England and back again, Lahiri charts the emotional voyages of characters seeking love beyond the barriers of nations, cultures, religions and generations. Imbued with the sensual details of both Indian and American cultures, they also speak with universal eloquence and compassion to everyone who has ever felt like an outsider. Like the interpreter of the title story which was selected for both the O'Henry Award and The Best American Short Stories—

Lahiri translates between the ancient traditions of her ancestors and the sometimes baffling prospects of the New World.

Jhumpa Lahiri has addressed several issues in *The Interpreter of Maladies*. These issues can be categorized as under:

1. Issues of Diaspora
2. Class and Community Awareness
3. Gender Roles
4. The search for identity
5. Conjugal disharmony

The stories, themes thereby include marital difficulties, miscarriages, and the disconnection between first and second generation immigrants.

Although not all of the stories in *Interpreter of Maladies* are set in America, all of them deal with characters in diaspora of one sort or another. Very few essential characters in the book live in their original homeland, and if they do, they represent the first generation in their family born into a western culture. Lahiri provides a very vivid peek into the Indian diaspora, which has been written about by so many authors in their own different ways.

The job that Mr. Kapasi, the protagonist of Jhumpa Lahiri's title story had found thankless for so many years, gets a shot in the arm when Mrs. Das finds it interesting. But the humble interpreter who earned extra by working as a driver cum guide during the weekends, becomes Lahiri's mirror to reflect Mrs. Das's own unfulfilled emotional life, beset in a country far from her own. Unlike many other diaspora writers, Lahiri's depiction of Indian milieu or Indianness of thought has a lot more realism which lets her readers relate more to both sides of the spectrum.

In the first of her stories, "A Temporary Matter", she has kept the milieu entirely in the mainstream American surroundings of Boston, while Shobha and Sukumar, the protagonist couple had their Indianness locked in with their depression but behind closed doors after the unfortunate birth of their still born baby. Quite conversely, the title story has been set in the traditional backdrop of Puri — one of the few major Indian centres of tradition and worship, and Konark, which has excellent carvings depicting conjugal life. And it is in this milieu that Mrs. Das finds her interpreter of maladies, to whom she is able to narrate untold chapters of her life — the discontent in marriage, the adultery and relief in trusting a man for the first time in eight years whom she considers being talented enough. Of course Mr. Kapasi has no cure for what ails Mrs. Das or himself. Lahiri's subtle bitter sweet ending is characteristic of the collection as a whole. Yet, the situations, Lahiri's characters face from unhappy marriages to civil war go beyond borders and cultures.

In the last story "The Third And Final Continent", one finds through the protagonist what perhaps Lahiri had set out to convey: "There are times I am bewildered by each mile I have travelled, each meal I have eaten, each person I have known, each room in which I have slept."[1] It is this universal experience that sets the book apart from the rest and relates to human experiences of love, despair, domicile and most importantly, being at a distance from one own's country.

The issues of diaspora is related to the search for identity. Lahiri deals most prolifically with the crisis of identity, as defined by the self, by others, by location and by circumstance. In Lahiri's stories, everything including gender, homeland, geography, occupation and role within community can act in determining and qualifying identity. Lahiri brings up interesting questions as to what can and cannot act as agents in the determination of identity, and many of her characters struggle against or conform to outside influences that have effects on self-definition and outside definition.

In "A Temporary Matter", the wife, Shobha, is an editor who has recently thrown herself into her work as an editor. Instead of having dinner with her husband, Shukumar, Shobha avoids him as much as possible, watching game shows or proofreading files "with her arsenal of coloured pencils at hand (8). It is noted that Shukumar and Shoba had become experts at avoiding each other in their three bedroom house" (4). Shoba has effectively edited elements of her own life following the miscarriage she suffered. Shukumar's identity as Indian is forged almost entirely from Americanised sources. We find out that "It wasn't until his father died, in his last year of college, that the country began to interest him, and he studied its history from the course books as if it were any other subject" (12). To create an identity based on books and a prefabricated hyphenated identification category mapped by America is not really possible.

In 'Sexy' Dev, a Bengali shows Miranda a map in *The Economist* to define where he is from and, thus, who he is. Dev chooses to define himself in terms of geographical boundaries as opposed to feelings of nationality. He tells her the political history of his home country is "nothing (she'll) ever need to worry about" (84).

The search for identity is highlighted also in the story "This Blessed house". Sanjeev dislikes his wife's collection of Christian paraphernalia from the time she begins discovering the treasures in their new house. However, the gleaming bust of Christ is the straw that breaks the camel's back. "He hated that it was in his house, and that he owned it. Unlike the other things they'd found, this contained dignity, solemnity beauty even. But to his surprise these qualities made him hate it all the more"(157). Sanjeev's sense of self or national self is threatened.

National identity and geographical boundaries are in conflict in the story "When Mr. Pirzada came to Dine". Lilia's father tells her in regard to Mr. Pirzada, "More importantly, Mr. Pirzada is no longer considered Indian — Dacca no longer belongs to us" (25). It raises the question whether national identity can change with a change in physical boundaries. Age and generation are interpreted as a function of identity in "The Third and Final Continent". A specific notion of home necessarily creates identity and even vice versa. Lahiri strongly feels, "A bicultural upbringing is a rich but imperfect thing."

Lahiri takes up the issue of class and community in India in two of the stories of *Interpreter of Maladies*. Both these stories "A Real Durwan" and "The Treatment of Bibi Haldar" focus specifically on the plight of the lower classes (usually in that section of the social strata because of forced diaspora and political struggle). She depicts the community as having an integral function when it comes to the lower classes making decisions and creating, within themselves, smaller hierarchies.

The opinions and generalizations made by the community in "A Real Durwan" have a great effect on how Boori Ma acts and interprets her own identity and class status. Much of her eccentric behaviour is excused because of her age. "Boori Ma's mouth is full of ashes, but she is the victim of changing times' was the refrain of old Mr. Chaterjee" (72). The generation gap and the fictionalization of a previous life style are underlined in "A Real Durwan." "The Treatment of Bibi Haldar" tells the story of a young woman with an unexplainable disease. Bibi is subjected to numerous doctors and their countless remedies for illness. Bibi's life is described "as an encounter with one fruitless antidote after another" (159). Within these fruitless antidotes a direct connection can be made between Bibis illness and the way she is treated by her family and community as well as the doctors.

Lahiri often toys with the reversal of gender roles, especially as they relate to husband and wife roles within marriages. Whereas in India a strict set of guidelines dictates how husbands and wives act both publicly and privately, in America, such guidelines are not as clear-cut and often, are thrown out altogether. Lahiri's married characters often deal with confusions of marriage roles in relation to cooking, working outside the home, and bearing children. According to Lahiri's generalisations of Indian marital culture, women are solely responsible for cooking and doing household chores, as well as becoming completely domesticated with the arrival of children. Men are, according to such guidelines, responsible for working and providing their families with a monetary income.

Most of Lahiri's characters, specifically the ones in diaspora, must cope with new and sometimes shockingly different gender stereotypes and roles in their new homeland. Generation gaps, culture shock upon moving away from the 'homeland' and questions of sexuality play their roles in Lahiri's interpretations of gender and what it means to Indians in diaspora.

In "A Temporary Matter" Shukumar and Shoba represent a possible reversal of gender roles in marriage. Shukumar is the stay-at-home student who does the cooking and cleaning, he is blamed in part for the miscarriage, whereas in India, the mother would bear the full responsibility. The generational difference that exists between the sexes is apparent in "A Temporary Matter".

Twinkle, the wife in "This Blessed House" is characterised as "excited and delighted by little things, like tasting a new flavour of ice-cream, or dropping a letter in a mailbox. It was a quality he did not understand. It made him feel stupid , as if the world contained hidden wonders he could not anticipate or see. He looked at her face, which, it occurred to him had not grown out of its girlhood..." (142). The image of sustained girlhood is admired in a wife in India. In marital relationships, women are expected to make docile home makers as twinkle attempts to be. Her girlish charm is not, however, a quality Sanjeev an Indian husband in diaspora in America admires or even tolerates in his wife. The gender stereotypes and more specifically, the husband-wife roles within Diasporan culture are in a dilemma or redefined. Indian immigrants living under the garb of American culture and life too have become Americanised.

The erosion of ethical values has led to a total collapse of older family values. Conjugal disharmony is thus an offshoot of the Americanised lifestyle. Jhumpa Lahiri's *Interpreter of Maladies* is an anthology of short stories showcasing the social realism of the American life of the Asian immigrants especially the Indians.

"The book definitely deserved a recognition of the stature of the Pulitzer, and lives up to the expectations of every Indian living away from home"[3] — Saurav Sen.

REFERENCES

1. Lahiri, Jhumpa *Interpreter of Maladies*, Harper Collins Publishers, India, 1999.
2. *Newsweek* March 6, 2006 issue.
3. Book Review, *Lahiri Jhumpa: Interpreter of Maladies*, Haughton and Miffin Publishers, Reviewed by Saurav Sen.

Technique of Portrayal in *Midnight's Children*

15

R.P. Pradhan

The structure of Salman Rushdie's *Midnight's Children* seems to be epical but its technique of story telling is different. According to Aristotle a story to be a story must have a definite beginning, a middle and an end. There is no such systematic story and sequence of events in this novel. Saleem Sinai, the hero and the narrator of the story says to Padma that he has got many stories to tell and his stories may leak into one another. His stories are all mixed up and also a bit confused. Again, the novelist also claims to have been influenced by the *Panchatantra* which is a classic of Indian stories. All these stories have oral features. All these tales have got some listeners. Rushdie seems to carry over the conventions of the oral feature of Indian stories. He creates an illusion of such type of story telling but he has to take resort to the written words. There is difference of the language of speech and the language of writing.

Again, Rushdie's method of story telling becomes different in another way also. On the one hand he makes an attempt to follow the tradition of Indian epical tales and on the other hand he is inspired by the postmodern and the postcolonial spirits of foreign writers. The result is that Rushdie appears to parody the elements of 'beginning' in the story. The beginning is related to the birth of the hero Saleem on the night of the 15th of August 1947 when India became free. However, this beginning is not so plain. It becomes complex and it is involved into the mazes of several stories which are digressive. The section of the birth of Saleem covers almost hundred pages. Pt. Nehru offers his congratulations in these words:

Dear Bay Saleem, My belated congratulations on the happy accident of your moment of birth! You are the newest bearer of that ancient face of India which is also eternally young. We shall be watching over your life with the closest attention: it will be, in a sense, the mirror of our own (122).

As Rushdie is an Indian migrant writer, his distance from his mother country gives him some advantage. He may be detached and objective in comparison with stay-at-home writers who look at the event from a very close quarter and cannot be fully disinterested in their description. Besides, Rushdie has also saved himself from the extremist attitude of some migrant writers who either praise their mother country in the superlative or satirise it vehemently. In this context he may attack Raja Rao for his nativist view of India. Rushdie exhibits a broad cosmopolitan attitude in several places in the novel. He cannot talk of Muslim culture of India rather he talks of Indian culture. However, his universal outlook has got limitations. In certain political events of India he has been more violent and aggressive so much so that he had to face a court case for defamation and was asked to expunge an entire chapter from the novel.

The novel deals with three major themes: Colonialism and neo-colonialism in India, History and the Individual and fragmentation, migrancy and memory. The novelist follows a direct and detached narrative technique in his approach towards British colonialism in India. Methwold in the beginning and his descendant Methwold in the end have been presented as symbols of colonial exploitation and have been attacked ruthlessly. Several ills of independent India have been attributed to the foul mischiefs played by the British rulers like Methwold. In the opinion of the novelist, if the foreigners like Methwold had not come to colonise and plunder India, India would have been a beautiful country.

In this context the novelist shows how the British colonialists created the myth that they had come to India to civilize the country. They also gave an impression that the British rule was good for the Indian people. The Indians were conditioned by and by into accepting the superiority of the British rulers. The Britishers framed the Indian educational systems, the India syllabus and introduced the books of studies from colonial perspectives. They wanted to create a class of educated men who might be mentally slave and English and who also could help them in the expansion of their empire. In this regard the novelist expresses that the real spirit of freedom lies in "decolonization of mind" which implies freedom of mind. Mere political transfer of power cannot offer real freedom.

Methwold, the manipulator of all these, has been presented as a morally degenerate character. He is personification of evil in the novel. He has been caricatured as a liar and also as a non-reliable person. His seduction of Vanita in the absence of her husband is an ugly blot on the character of a colonialist. Rushdie describes the "ravishing strides" of Methwold:

> Vanita was alone with the centre-parting, feeling it exert a pull on her fingers that was impossible to resist, and as Methwold sat immobile in a cane chair, wearing a light weight cream suit with a single rose in the lapel, she found herself approaching him, fingers outstretched, felt fingers touching hair, found centre-parting; and began to rumple it up. (103)

The narrator shows how in several colonies the British officers had seduced and raped the women of the poor and had left behind mixed products of their illegitimate union.

Saleem, the narrator of the story, is also the son of Methwold and Vanita. Being a bastard he had to live a tragic life. He is confronted with the situation of an exile from time to time. He becomes a homeless wanderer. His condition is sad and gloomy like that of an expatriate. His first exile comes when he loses the home of Vanita. Further it is discovered that his blood group does not belong to his father Ahmad or his mother. It makes possible his another exile and he is sent away to his uncle Hanif. This displacement gives him a deep shock and he never recovers from it. Again, the family moves from Bombay to Karachi, Saleem is exiled from Bombay. He loves this city very much: "I never forgive Karachi for not being Bombay." Such displacement leads to his disintegration.

In his description of the relation of history and the individual the novelist follows allegorical method. He has drawn a parallel between the life of Saleem and the history of independent India. Saleem's birth coincides with the moment of India's independence and the event makes the protagonist and free India as Siamese twins. Saleem is identified as the first child born in independent India and the story of his life becomes the history of free India. Saleem refers to his birth and the link of his destiny with the freedom of India:

> I was born in Doctor Narlikar's Nursing Home on August 15th, 1947. And the time? The time matters, too. Well then: at night. No, it's important to be more.... On the stroke of midnight, as a matter of fact. Clock-hands joined palms in respectful greeting as I came. Oh, spell it out, spell it out: at the precise instant of India's arrival at independence, I tumbled forth into the world. There were gasps. And, outside the window, fire-works and crowds. A few seconds later, my father broke his big toe; but his accident was a mere trifle when set beside what had befallen me in that benighted moment, because thanks to the occult tyrannies of those blandly saluting clocks I had been mysteriously handcuffed to history, my destinies indissolubly chained to those of my country.(9)

Several children might be born at that moment but Saleem alone carries within him the history of free India. The novelist maintains throughout the novel the close relation between personal events in Saleem's life and the life of his family with the political and historical events of free India. It is stated that Saleem was responsible for the language riots of 1950s. He played an important role in Indo-Pak war of 1971, he had been suffering much during the emergency of 1975.

The novelist also follows a flashback technique and describes how Saleem's grandparents Aziz and Naseem Sinai while going from Kashmir to Agra face the events of Jallianwallah Bagh massacre. The event refers to an ugly moment in the colonial history of India. The narrator presents a pictorial description:

As the fifty-one men march down the alleyway a tickle replaces the itch in my grandfather's nose. The fifty-one men enter the compound and take up positions, twenty-five to Dyer's right and twenty five to his left.... As Brigadier Dyer issues a command the sneeze hits my grandfather full in the face. Yaahh-thooo! He sneezes and falls forward.... Thereby saving his life.... Red stuff stains his shirt. There are screams now and sobs and the strange chattering continues. More and more people seem to have stumbled and fallen on top of my grandfather.(36)

The novelist describes how General Dyer goes on firing and shooting the people in a brutal manner. Aziz feels suffocated in the situation and falls down. His shirt is stained with the blood of the dying people. Further Rushdie comes to the Indo-Pak war of 1965 and narrates how Saleem's parents, grandparents and aunt are killed when the airforces of India bombard Rawalpindi.

Saleem tells us that there is a close link between him and India. His face resembles the map of India:

> Baby-snaps reveal that my large moon-face was too large; too perfectly round. Something lacking in the region of the chin. Fair chain curved across my features-but birthmarks disfigured it; dark stains spread down my western hairline; a dark patch covered my eastern ear... Baby Saleem's nose: it was monstrous; and it ran. (124)

In an interview Rushdie also refers to the big nose of Saleem which is likened to a particular organ of India which is hanging into the sea.

Saleem cherishes a notion that the history of his life is symbolic of the history of India. In an ironical manner the novelist shows that Saleem is caught in an illusion in his identification with India. Really, he is a poor victim of the colonial and the neo-colonial situations. He realizes the state of contrast:

> From ayah to widow, I've been the sort of person to whom things have been done; but Saleem Sinai, perennial victim, persists in seeing himself as protagonist.... (237)

Thus, Saleem is no longer India or its history, he is a poor sufferer. He has lost his family, his root and has become a non-entity. He realizes that he has been assuming the role of responsibility in a false manner. His identification with India, its history and its destiny is also false. He has been received into believing that being a midnight child he has got a special role to play in the events of India. His mental illusion causes his fall from the highest peak to the lowest level in the Pakistani army's non-existent unit.

Saleem is idealized at the outset. He reads the mind of other people and evaluates them. He finds that out of several gifted midnight children three are outstanding, Saleem, Shiv and Parvati-the-witch who is the most talented female child of midnight. She was "born a mere seven seconds after midnight on August 15th had been given the powers of the true adept, the illuminatus, the genuine gifts of conjuration and sorcery, the art which required no artifice" (200). The third is Shiva who is also born "on the stroke of midnight" and has been given the gifts of war. He is a close friend and also an adversary of Saleem. Each of the three is given with supernatural power or superhuman qualities. However, in the end they are all destroyed. These and other children of the midnight differ in their ideas and fall a natural victim to jealousy, strife, narrow outlook, regional and communal feelings and in that way they cause the disintegration of India into small linguistic states.

Padma is both friend and beloved of Saleem. In the end Saleem marries her. She is uneducated, she listens to the story narrated by Saleem. She belongs to the working class. Her nature is assertive. She is open and frank on all matters. She wants to disappear from the life of Saleem but Saleem keeps her engaged in his stories. She makes several queries and renders the narrative entertaining. The novelist follows narrative technique in the delineation of her character.

Rushdie introduces a large number of common people who remain socially marginalised. In this respect he falls in line with the Marxist thinker Mulk Raj Anand who has made Bakha, a low caste person as the hero of his *Untouchable*. Tai, the boatman is the most attractive commoner in Midnight's Children. He is a regular talker and weaves fantastic stories for the child Aziz. Lifafa Das is another common character. He is a man of broad outlook. During the period of riots he visits a Muslim locality and is identified as a Hindu by a small girl. The crowd is instigated into chasing him but Saleem's mother Amina gives him shelter and stands between him and angry crowd and his life is saved. Lifafa Das, Tai and Saleem's Ayah are all common characters and play vital role in the novel. Rushdie has made the commoners memorable.

Another important technique which has been followed in the novel is that of magic realism. Magic realism is the product of Latin America and it has spread all over the world. Salman Rushdie follows the magic realist mode in this novel. The magic realist novels of the west move away from the world which is considered to be real. They are set in an unreal world which shows the interplay of fantasy and realism. The magic realist makes use of fantasy and in this regard he calls in question the place of reality in art. His combination of fantasy and realism is a reaction against the conception of 19th century realism. The magic realist cannot satisfy the demand that fiction should imitate reality all the time. He challenges the notion of traditional reality in the realm of art. He is inspired by the spirit of science in discovering the nature of reality. In the opinion of the magic realist fiction should become the form of investigating the nature of truth and not of imitating reality.

Midnight's Children has been written in the magic realist form. In this spirit it calls in question the nature of reality. According to Rushdie history is a lie and it might be twisted into any form. Saleem "is cutting history to suit himself." He commits so many errors regarding the Indian history. His errors are also mythological such as the Ganesha error. Saleem is very boastful of his knowledge of Hindu religion but his error regarding Hindu mythology is very great and therefore he cannot be trusted as a narrator. Again he cannot be called a detached and a correct observer. He has got a vested interest in exaggerating certain events and in that way he wants to become the hero of the story.

Saleem cannot be relied on as an authentic narrator. Some of his facts are wrong and erroneous. It is because he has taken the help of memory and remembered truth. The selection and the interpretation of facts in history by a writer may not be objective. Saleem's method shows that facts may be selected and may also be distorted to promote certain interests. Certain facts which serve the interest of certain groups may be brought into full light and other important facts may be ignored. History may be official and it may hide the facts. What appears to be fact is really a story. The magic realist technique of Rushdie is a strategy to overcome the limitations of historical descriptions. There is strange mixture of the probable and the improbable in the novel. The natural and the supernatural are mixed together through the stories of Saleem and Padma. There are fortune tellers who prophecy the birth of a son, there are saints who wait for the coming of the Blessed One, there are little girls who speak in the language of birds and cats. All such fantastic things have been described in a vivid manner. Hence, there is fusion of the real and the fantastic.

The handling of the Hindu myths and traditions in relation to characters is an integral part of Rushdie's technique. It has gone into a good deal of criticism because his attidue is parodic and irreverent. Rushdie has been called a trickster and an impostor for his dealing with the myths. In addition to Ganesh myth Saleem makes use of several other Indian myths in a careless and rebellious manner. His play on the name of Padma is also unpleasant. The main myth is that of Shiva. Rushdie presents the destructive side of Shiva. He is intended to banish evil from the world but in the novel Shiva degenerates into evil force whose aim is to destroy Saleem. Rushdie has not done justice to the myth of Shiva and uses it in his way as it suits him and in that way turns it upside down. His spirit is closely connected with the postmodern attitude for playful treatment of serious religious things. Rushdie protests the unique character of "Indianess". The postmodern writer cannot feel at home in the world of tradition. Such ironical treatment of Indian myths is not the exclusive right of Rushdie, others have also done the same. Such attitude towards Indian myths reflects the contemporary spirit of the west.

In certain other myths the description of Rushdie is full of humour and wit. It cannot be declared as something unpleasant. His description of the meditation and mystical pose of Buddha presents the finest example of a technique which is plain, expressive, philosophical at the same time:

> Once upon a time, a prince, unable to bear the suffering of the world, became capable of not-living-in-the-world as well as living in it; he was present, but also absent; his body was in one place, but his spirit was elsewhere. In ancient India, Gautama the Buddha sat enlightened under a tree at Gaya; in the deer park at Sarnath he taught others to abstract themselves from worldly sorrows and achieve inner peace. (349-50)

Because of its new technique *Midnight's Children* cannot be classified into a particular genre of novel writing. There is a strange mixture of fact and fiction, myth and history, story telling and conversation. A particular critic has called it historiographic metafiction. It is a kind of fiction which has got the traits of history and metafiction. As regards history the novel does not follow the direct line of history. It deals with events that seem probable but they are not true. Metafiction challenges the idea of realism which is regarded as the only way of writing fiction. Historiographic metafiction is quite in keeping with the spirit of postmodernism. Rushdie writes with the postmodern outlook but he also wants to become an oriental storyteller like that of *Panchatantra*. The technique becomes complicated because it combines the spirit of postmodernism and postcolonialism in several ways.

The followers of the genre of historiographic metafiction break the barriers of history and fiction. They want to show how writers make up their stories and how history is also made up in the form of story. Their method is that of parody. Rushdie wants to show that historical incidents are fictitious and hence there can be no demarcation line between history and fiction. Reality is also a made-up thing. The postmodern fiction writer challenges the view that art can present reality in an accurate manner. In the view of such writer the historian chooses only those facts that promote his interest and make an appeal to him. The postmodern fiction sticks to the idea that reality is a thing of our own making. Saleem presents only those incidents which can make him a hero. India presented by Saleem is India of his own version and imagination but it is also true. He shows that he is not interested in writing the history of India. He is keen to show how a man "filters" reality. Memory of Saleem takes into account all that is pleasant to him and it discards all that is unpleasant to him.

To sum up Rushdie on the one hand follows the method of oral narrative in the portrait of characters. On the other hand he also assimilates the trends of postmodernism and postocolonialism. In that way he has set up a new genre of fiction writing in *Midnight's Children*. The theme of the problem of writing a novel runs throughout the novel. The contrast is glaring. The postmodern fiction has got no story to tell. The ancient Indian genius has been a story telling genius. Rushdie seems to take the best of the two worlds, the oriental and the occidental. He has brought about a fusion of the two while inventing something from his own side. That is his uncommon original technique.

REFERENCE

Rushdie, Salman. *Midnight's Children*, Vintage, 1995.

Criticism

Postmodernism: An Overview

16

R.N. Rai

World War II (1939-45) led to the emergence of changed national identities. Whereas England was relegated to the background, America emerged as a super power, though uncertain of its national as well as international role. Passing through the traumas of cold war, U.S.A. moved towards anti-communism, consumerism, conformity and corporate bureaucracy. It pleaded for the emergence of advanced capitalist societies, liberation movements, protection of civil rights, gay and feminist protest. It resulted in the emergence of new kind of society which was variously known as post-industrial society, consumer society and media society. It also led to the arrival of "multinational capitalism" and "automobile culture". There was a radical shift in the perception of 'man' who was now regarded as a being, situated as any other object in the world. Even if we look at postmodernism mainly as a form of Americanisation of the world, postmodernism cannot be regarded as a homogeneous phenomenon, as even in America various forms of ideological and political conflicts are still going on.

In the fifties and early sixties the term 'Postmodernism' was briefly used in critical essays in order to register, says Peter Brooker in his Introduction to *Modernism/Postmodernism* (1994), "tremors in cultural values" (2). Since the early eighties not only the literary theorists but political scientists, sociologists, geographers, philosophers and media theorists also started using 'postmodernism' as a key term in order to explain the contemporary consciousness. However, even in 1980 the American writer, John Barth in the Article "The Literature of Replenishment; Postmodernist Fiction", regarded postmodernism as a term "awkward and faintly epigonic, suggestive less of a vigorous or even interesting new direction...." (66).

Serious literary critical debate about postmodernism, however, began with the publication of Jean-Francois Lyotard's *The Postmodern Condition* in 1979 (translated into English in 1984). Lyotard's declaration of the collapse of grand narratives and metanarratives displaced the holistic certainties of structuralist thought. From the very beginning postmodernism was opposed to the decorums and hierarchies of the literary establishment and pleaded for an open, randomised and popular forms of art such as poetry, music, architecture and film. Referring to the multiple manifestations of postmodernism Peter Brooker has rightly remarked:

> Postmodernism, we can say, splices high with low culture, it raids and parodies past art, it questions all absolutes, it swamps reality in a culture of recycled images, it has to do with deconstruction, with consumerism, with television and the information society, with the end of communism. (3)

By the end of the eighties, postmodernism came to be used in three broad contexts—in the context of the cultural epoch through which we were passing and which was largely viewed in apocalyptic terms; as an aesthetic practice which was seen as co-extensive with the commodified surfaces of this culture; as a development in thought which questions the discourse of modernity or the established assumptions of enlightenment. We are made aware of this fact that modernity is now coming to an end and we are entering into a new world of information technology, global economics and consumerist approach towards life which erode the stability of concepts such as nation, state or essential human nature. Referring to the salient features of postmodern age, Patricia Waugh in his Introduction to *Postmodernism* (1994) has rightly pointed out:

> In such a world consciousness is a drift, unable to anchor itself to any universal ground of justice, truth or reason on which the ideals of modernity had been founded in the past...... Art becomes not so much an expression of human spirit but another commodity. Like Knowledge, therefore, it can no longer be critical but only functional. (5)

Postmodernism has led to the constant growth of multinational capitalism resulting in the faceless expansion of global market and unlimited scope of electronic media. This process of change has drastically altered our social and psychic conditions and produced a 'massively coded world of relentless commodification'. In this fast changing 'depthless' world old distinctions and orientations are disappearing. There is a loss of emotional attachment and objective assessment. Human beings are deprived of historical consciousness and they are gradually becoming incapable of grasping the socio-cultural totality of human existence. Referring to the disappearance of a sense of history in the contemporary society, Fredric Jameson in "Postmodernism and Consumer society", published in *Modernism/Postmodernism* ed. by Peter Brooker has drawn our attention to the way in which "our entire contemporary social system has little by little begun to lose its capacity to retain its own past, has begun to live in a perpetual present and in a perpetual change that obliterates tradition of the kind which all earlier social formations have had in one way or another to preserve" (179). Electronic media is playing a very important role in leading us to our 'historical amnesia'. Media messages saturate the cultural field so completely with an overload of information that the masses are converted into an inert and silent majority. The very transition to postmodernism has rightly been described by Brooker as the "shift from questions of epistemology (ways of knowing) to questions of ontology (ways of being and acting in the world)" (21). In postmodernism, there is no possibility of a unified self, a narrative perspective or a revival of history. Past is recoverable only as pastiche which is, like parody, the imitation of a peculiar or unique style, the wearing of a stylistic mask, speech in a dead language.

The socio-economic and technological changes have brought about a marked shift into 'the heteroglossia of intercultural exchange'. Popular forms of art are blended or blurred together. Postmodernism has obliterated the hierarchical distinctions between 'high' and 'low' culture. The new democratic art has bridged the gap between high and mass culture and dispensed with the elitist 'autonomy' of modernism. Irving Howe has condemned this tendency as a debased commodification of the aesthetic, whereas John Baith has regarded it as the effect for the replacement of 'literatures of exhaustion' by the 'essentially parodic literature of replenishment'. Postmodernism is now used to express, says Patricia Waugh in his introduction to *Postmodernism*, "the sense of a new cultural epoch in which distinction between critical and functional knowledge break down as capitalism, in its latest consumerist phase, invades everything including the aesthetic, the post-colonial world and the unconscious, leaving no remaining oppositional space"(3).

In his article "The culture of Postmodernism', published in *Theory, Culture and Society*, 2,3 (1985), Ihab Hassan has drawn our attention to some of the distinguishing features between Modernism and Postmodernism which are given below:

Modernism	**Postmodernism**
Romanticism/Symbolism	Pataphysics/Dadaism
Form (Conjunctive, Closed)	Antiform (disjunctive, open)
Purpose	Play
Design	Chance
Hierarchy	Anarchy
Mastery/ Logos	Exhaustion/ Silence
Art object/Finished work	Process/Performance/ Happening
Distance	Participation
Creation/ Totalisation / Synthesis	Decreation/Deconstruction/ Antithesis
Presence	Absence
Centering	Dispersal
Genre /Boundary	Text/Intertext
Semantics	Rhetoric
Paradigm	Syntagm
Hypotaxis	Parataxis
Metaphor	Metonymy

Selection	Combination
Root/Depth	Rhizome/Surface
Interpretation/ Reading	Against interpretation/ Misreading
Signified	Signifier
Lisible (Readerly)	*Scriptible* (Writerly)
Narrative/*Grande Histoire*	Anti-narrative/ *Petite Histoire*
Master Code	Idiolect
Symptom	Desire
Type	Mutant
Genital/ Phallic	Polymorphous/Androgynous
Paranoia	Schizophrenia
Origin/Cause	Difference-Differance/ Trace
God The Father	The Holy Ghost
Metaphysics	Irony
Determinacy	Indeterminacy
Transcendence	Immanence (123)

It is not possible to agree with the scheme of differentiation in its totality and it has rightly been criticised by some critics like Christine Brooke Rose and Susan Rubin Suleiman for its 'categorical' and 'local' inconsistencies. However, Hassan remains committed to his view of modernism as 'centred' and of postmodernism as 'decentred'. The 'decentred' postmodernism is also characterised by the terms 'indeterminacy' and 'immanence' which are comprised of sub-tendencies such as 'heterodoxy', 'pluralism', 'eclecticism', 'deformation', and 'difference', etc. In his article "Ideas of cultural change", published in *Innovation/ Renovation: New Perspectives on the Humanities*, Hassan explains 'immanence' as "the capacity of the mind to generalise itself in the world...and so become more and more, immediately, its own environment" (29). Postmodernism which is regarded as the enemy of totalising vision, tries to transcend postmodern heterodoxy, and ironically promises a global oneness, the 'one human universe'.

Postmodernism dencentred ethnocentric, epistemological and cultural models and placed central emphasis on subordinated or marginalised discourses and traditions. It put emphasis on the issues of otherness such as the issues of Afro-Americans, Native Americans, women and gays, etc. It has brought the repressed and the marginal into view and the unvoiced into hearing. It is a debatable issue whether marginalised groups are empowered in the postmodernist era or lost in a centreless world. One thing, however, is certain that emphasis has now been certainly placed on the particular, multiple and the heterogeneous. In the essay "Radical Democracy: Modern or Postmodern", published in *Universal Abandon? The Politics of Postmodernism*, Chantal Mouffe has rightly remarked:

> Radical democracy demands that we acknowledge difference, the particular, the multiple, the heterogeneous—in effect everything that has been excluded by the concept of man in the abstract. Universalism is not rejected but particularized: what is needed is a new kind of articulation between the universal and the particular (36).

Postmodernism preserves multiplicity and local cultures and firmly refuses to submerge differences into universalism. It represents a genuine democratisation of art and provides scope for internal disruption.

If Marxism is regarded as the radical political discourse of modernity, Feminism is regarded as the paradigmatic political discourse of postmodernity. Pointing out the significance of Feminism in the postmodernist discourse, Laura Kipnis in "Feminism: The Political Conscience of Postmodernism", published in *Universal Abandon? The Politics of Postmodernism* has stated: "Its affirmation of the absence, the periphery, and the other-spaces in which the position of women is structurally and politically inscribed—has more current political credibility than Marxism..." (208). In Feminist Theory, the concept of the periphery, the absence and the margin draws our attention to the fact that women are not regarded as class or caste but as colony. In the capitalist society or even elsewhere we find women in colonial relationship to men. Feminist discourses have exposed some of the most disguised contradictions and limitations of the Enlightenment thought by articulating issues of sexual difference. Feminist discourses contradict the principle of sameness of Enlightenment thought. Feminism exposes, says Patricia Waugh in "Modernism, Postmodernism, Feminism: Gender and Autonomy Theory", published in *Postmodernism*, "the ways in which this 'universal' principle is contradicted by Enlightenment's construction of a public/private split which consigns women to the 'private' realm of feeling, domesticity, the body, in order to clarify a 'public' realm of reason as masculine. In this sense, at least feminism can be seen to be an intrinsically 'postmodern' discourse" (189).

Postmodern art and theory deconstructed the liberal individual and dissolved the traditional aesthetic conceptualisations of character. It tried to reexamine the Enlightenment concepts of subjectivity as autonomous self-determination. It defined the human individual without making any reference to history, traditional values, God or nation. Postmodernism also made attempts to formulate, says P. Waugh, "strategies for narrative disruption of traditional stories and construction of new identity scripts, without embracing its more extreme nihilistic or pragmatist implications" (190). It is evident from the appearance of new theory and new movements in art and culture that poststructuralism and postmodernism are partners in the same paradigm.

In the postmodernist era, the individual is deprived of historical consciousness and hence he is incapable of imbibing the interpretative grasp which will give him an understanding of socio-cultural totality. The alienated individual under monopoly capitalism has now become 'schizophrenic'. He has lost all sense of authenticity and has developed a sense of withdrawl from real human existence. The schizophrenic individual is placed in such a condition in which he is cast adrift, says Peter Brooker, "in the perpetual present of a superficial centreless world, replete with ever new, recycled images or representations" (22).

The 'schizophrenic' tendency of postmodernism has been linked by Fredric Jameson with a pervasive nostalgia. In the opinion of P. Waugh "it is the nostalgia which produces the desire to fragment, the impossible yearning for the lost (imaginary) object of desire which issues in the frustrated and atavistic smashing of the ideal object" (192). The violent face of postmodernism is the nihilistic philosophy which suggests that if things are fragmenting, let them fragment completely. That is why Nietzsche is often regarded as the first postmodernist. It is of course very difficult to ascertain whether extreme fragmentation or dehumanisation is being used as a parodic mode of critique or as an extension of fragmented and dehumanised world. Postmodern aesthetic forms very often draw on modes of irony, parody, multiplicity and fragmentation.

In the opinion of Fredric Jameson, postmodernism is nothing but the natural development of the 'schizophrenic condition of late capitalism'. Patricia Waugh, however, does not agree with the view and suggests that the postmodernism may be regarded as a *fin-de-siecle* parody, or caricature, of a dualism that is inherent in the Western philosophical traditions. In his view, "the autonomous transcendent self of German idealism, Enlightenment humanism, European Romanticism and realist aesthetics and the impersonally fragmented self of postmodernism are products of same cultural tradition" (199).

We all agree that postmodernism is much concerned with the expression of the fragmentary of schizoid self. Either it explores the fragmentary world or tries to discover modes which will fracture and dissolve the old unities. Contemporary scholars and critics are so much fascinated by the idea of fragmentation that Barthelme goes to the extent of declaring: 'Fragments are the only forms I trust'. Commenting upon the significance of fragmentation in postmodernism, P. Waugh has remarked: "Fragmentation into atoms becomes the means of escaping patriarchal surveillance and control of the pleasure principle. Fragmentation and dehumanisation are part of a postmodern assault on the bondage of thought to regulative ideals such as 'unity' and 'truth' (192). In the context of apocalyptic postmodernism it is quite possible that "its schizophrenic fragmentation is a response to a continuing obsession with an impossible ideal" (194).

Postmodernism is opposed to the predominance of metanarratives or 'grand narratives' which have in fact broken down in the contemporary era. In his Introduction to *Postmodernism,* Patricia Waugh has frankly stated: "Postmodernism, tends to claim an abandonment of all metanarratives which could legitimate foundations for truth. And more than this, it claims that we neither need them nor are they any longer desirable" (5). The credit for the proclamation of the collapse of the Enlightenment 'grand narratives' goes to Lyotard who in *The Postmodern Condition* (1979) made an announcement to this effect, though the idea was already familiar in the thought of Nietzsche, Wittegenstein and Foucault among others. What led to the collapse of the significance of metanarratives? It was in fact on account of, says P. Waugh, "the demise of structuralism and the development of a poststructuralist critique of systems of knowledge which assume a stable depth/surface relation such that a hidden 'core' of truth may be archeologically uncovered with the appropriate tools of excavation and casually related to an apparently contingent surface" (5-6). Poststructuralism denounced the idea that knowledge is the reflection of truth and that a stable foundation for truth for it may be discovered in God, History or Reason. In the works of Derrida, Lacan, and the later Barthes the signifier was given priority over the signified. It was clearly stated that the meaning of the text is radically indeterminate, as all the texts are implicated in an endless intertextuality. Hence Lyotard suggested that we should acknowledge the exhaustion of metanarratives and advocated for context-specific agreements, heterogeneity, pragmatism and incommensurability. Totality of meaning was no longer acceptable as totalities were equated with totalitarianism and terror. Search for universal concept was regarded as an imperialist motive. The text of a postmodern writer need not be governed by pre-established norms and it need not be judged by the familiar categories of the text. It would evolve its own category and would be judged by its own norms.

Another distinguishing feature of postmodernism is the effacement of the older categories of genre and discourse in contemporary theory. A generation ago there used to be different discourses of different academic disciplines such as philosophy, sociology, political science or literary criticism. Today, the older distinction has disappeared and now we have a kind of writing which is simply known as theory that is all or none of them at once. Where can we place the work of Michael Foucault for instance? Is it to be known as philosophy, history, political science or social theory? Such a theoretical discourse is of course a remarkable manifestation of postmodernism.

WORKS CITED

Barth, John. *The literature of Replenishment: Postmodernist Fiction*. The Atlantic 245, 1, 1980.

Brooker, Peter ed. *Modernism/Postmodernism*. London: Longman, 1994.

Hassan, Ihab. "The Culture of Postmodernism", *Theory, Culture and Society*. 2, 3, 1985.

Hassan, Ihab. "Ideas of Cultural Change", *Innovation/ Renovation: New Perspectives on the Humanities* ed. Ihab Hassan and Sally Hassan. Madison: University of Wisconsin Press, 1983.

Jameson, Frederic. "Postmodernism and Consumer Society", *Modernism/ Postmodernism* ed. Peter Brooker. London: Longman, 1994.

Kipnis, Laura. "Feminism: The Political Conscience of Postmodernism" *Universal Abandon? The Politics of Postmodernism* ed. Andrew Ross. Edinburg: Edinburg University press, 1989.

Moufee, Chantal. "Radical Democracy: Modern or Postmodern *Universal Abandon? The Politics of Postmodernism* ed. Andrew Ross. Edinburg: Edinburg University Press, 1989.

Waugh, Patricia ed. *Postmodernism*. London: Edward Arnold, 1994.

Postmodernism: Its Meaning and Significance

17

G. Rai and Sunita Rai

Postmodernity and postmodernism are used interchangeably. It is wrong and unethical. Postmodernity is the time or condition in which we find ourselves. Postmodernism designates various schools and movements it has produced.

The term postmodernism was first used by Arnold Toynbee in 1939 in *A Study of History* to express his idea of a postmodern age of Western history. The term gained currency and was extensively used by sociologists, philosophers and art critics in course of time. The word is ambiguous and has been used with a great deal of imprecision. It has acquired a wide range of attributions and meanings in academic debates. In general terms, it describes a mood or condition of radical indeterminacy and a tone of self-conscious skepticism towards previous certainties in personal, intellectual and political life. Two influential arguments of postmodernism are associated with J. F. Lyotard and Jean Baudrillard. It is felt that the grand narratives of human progress and liberation, rooted in the Enlightenment thought, have lost credibility, and that a culture of detached media images has come to suffocate and out alone the real world, ousting old-fashioned worries about the relationship of the images to the real.

Postmodernism is a movement defining itself by reference to and reaction against modernity. The 'post' has the sense of a simple succession. The 'post' indicates something like a conversion—a new direction from the previous one. Now this idea of a linear chronology is itself perfectly modern. The very idea of modernity is closely co-related with the principle that it is both possible and necessary to break with tradition and institute absolutely new ways of living and thinking. The word modern in its latin form 'modernus' was used for the first time in the late fifth century in order to distinguish the present which had become officially Christian from the Roman and Pagan past. With varying content, the term again and again expresses the consciousness of an epoch that relates itself to the past of antiquity, in order to view itself as the result of a transition from the old to the new. People in the 12th and 17th centuries called themselves modern. That is to say the term 'modern' appeared and reappeared.

Postmodern experience is widely held to stem from a profound sense of ontological uncertainly. Human shock in the face of the unimaginable (pollution, holocaust, the death of the subject) results in a loss of fixed points of reference. Neither the world nor the self any longer possesses unity, coherence or meaning. They are radically decentred. There is no consensus among scholars as regards the meaning of postmodernism. It has been described both as an extension and intensification of modernism and as a reaction against modernism. While it has been treated by some critics as a distinctively American phenomenon, others have applied the term both to European writing and to contemporary Avant-garde movements in the non-literary arts. Linda Hutcheon describes the postmodern as

> the contemporary phenomena that uses and abuses, installs and then subverts, the very concepts it challenges—be it in literature, painting, sculpture, film, video, dance, television, music, philosophy, aesthetic theory, psychoanalysis, linguistic or historiography.[1]

Jean-Francois Lyotard characterises the postmodern as possessing "an incredulity toward metanarrative."[2] Craig Owens calls it "a crisis of cultural authority, specifically of the authority vested in European culture and its institutions."[3] Postmodernism is best seen as an extension of modernism. Stanley Aronowitz defines postmodernism "as a rejection of reason as a foundation of human affairs."[4] Neil Larson calls postmodernism "a form of irrationalism.[5]

Postmodernism is a reaction against the project of enlightenment, i.e. human development is based on logic and knowledge of science and not on religion. Ihab Hassan supports postmodernism and criticises enlightenment in the name of a new world free from the repressive effect of perfection. Deconstruction challenges the traditional ideology of the West and sympathises with the political and linguistic and other minorities and contains a ray of hope for Hassan for cultural and political revolution. The enlightenment project and the twentieth century scientific rationalism that grew out of it was not only a philosophical effort, then, but an ideology of progress, a belief in "linear progress, absolute truths and rational planning of ideal social orders." A metanarrative is a story of mythic proportions, a story big enough and meaningful enough to pull together philosophy and research, politics and art, relate them to one another, and above all give them a unifying sense of direction. Lyotard cited as examples the Christian religious story of God's will being worked out on earth, the Marxist political story of class-conflict and revolution, and the Enlightenment intellectual story of rational progress. Loytard defined postmodern era as a time of "incredulity toward metanarratives." Lyotard does not mean that all people have ceased to believe in all stories but rather that the stories are not working so well any more because these are too many—'the centre cannot hold'. We are exposed to diverse and contradictory fragments of stories and the arts and sciences go their various ways. The Enlightenment pictured the human race as engaged in an effort towards universal moral and intellectual self-realisation, and so as the subject of a universal historical experience, it also postulated a universal human reason in terms of which social and political tendencies could be assessed as 'progressive' or otherwise. The goal of politics is defined as the realisation of reason in practice. Postmodernism rejects this picture; that is to say, it rejects the doctrine of the unity of reason. It refuses to conceive of humanity as a unitary subject striving towards the goal of perfect coherence or of perfect cohesion and stability. Lyotard, Alasdair Mac Intyre and Richard Rorty advocate pluralism in morals, politics and epistemology. They question the merit of consensus as a regulative ideal of discourse. The policy of working for it is objectionable on two counts: (i) it is historically outmoded (ii) it is misguided or sinister in its own right. The enlightenment project is seen as having produced a wide range of social and political disasters from modern warfare to nuclear threat and severe ecological crisis. The results of modernisation have been bureaucracy, oppression and misery as the Enlightenment narrative of liberation and equality has ground into its opposite. It is argued that revolution for social change and struggle for equality and liberation lead to new forms of oppression and exploitation.

Postmodernism is an exaltation of the irrational. The last quarter of the 19th century is the beginning of modernism and in a sense it also marks the beginning of postmodernism. Neitzsche and Heideggar, like other existentialists, are the philosophers of irrationalizm who do not believe in the universals of conventional philosophy. Monroe K. Spears observed that modernism began when Dionysus entered the city[7], i.e. the centre of civilisation of which rationalism is taken as the cornerstone. Thus, there is an element of irrationalism in modernism which is buttressed by the authority of Neitzsche and Freud, the two major influences on modernists. For Neitzsche, logic and morality are a hindrance in the will to power and therefore he detests Christianity which with its faith in moral perfection and spiritual values entails slave morality. For Freud, logic stands in the way of emotional fulfilment. This explains why people take so much delight in non-sense which has its roots in the feeling of freedom we enjoy, when we are able to abandon the straightjacket of logic. The irrationalism is idealised, by the postmodernists under the impression that reason is the mam trouble-maker, which has turned the conventional philosophers from Plato down to Kant; and Hegel upside down. Post-modernism designates logic, the legacy; of the Enlightenment, as authoritarian, patriarchal, and racist. Colonialism and Facism stemmed from the kind of hegemony that logic gives.

Postmodernism represents a new age in human history when the orthographic tradition is seriously threatened by the electronic media. The function of literature has been taken over by film and television which have also in the process appropriated various literary modes. At one stage of the cultural history of man, the oral tradition had given way to the written tradition. The living voice had yielded to the cold alphabets. And now for all practical purposes, television, taperecorder and computer have taken over the roles formerly played by books and libraries. We do not have any definite cultural seismograph of the change from the oral to the written. But the effect of the process of the replacement of the written by the electronic and the audio-visual, has been obviously very massive and pervasive. In French one meaning of 'poste' is 'television set'. Postmodernism in culture is 'postemodernism' or 'television culture' linking knowledge and experience, education and entertainment, and the auditory and the visual, in a manner unthinkable in my previous era. Baudrillard's message in the post 1970s include the loss of the real and of the appearance of the culture of hyper reality in which models determine the real. In the epoch of simulation, reality is gone for good and we are left only with appearance. According to Baudrillard, there is no longer a real external world to which signs can refer, there has been an implosion of image and reality. This implosion leads into the simulated non-space of hyper-reality. The real is now defined in terms of the media in which it moves. It is the image-creating postmodern communication technologies especially television—which proliferate self-generating, self-mirroring, depthless images. Experience now is superficial everywhere. It achieves its final Utopian form in the instantaneous abundance and banality of the American cultureless society, i.e. in Disneyland Baudriland's later writings—*Fatal Strategies*, *America*—are nihilistic. He sees postmodernity repeatedly in terms of the appearance of meaning inertia, exhaustion and endings, whether of history or subjectivity. Fukuyama similarly writes on the theme of the end of history following the fall of communism. For Baudrillard, everything is 'obscenely' on display, moving endlessly, transparently across a surface where there is no control or stabilizing depth. His most provocative recent proposal has been that the Gulf war was not a real war but a television war, a media event or spectacle. It is unreal war without the symptom of war. He sees in this episode the operation of a 'logic of deterrence, from hot to cold war, and so to fighting over 'the corpse of war'. War is caught up in the process of postmodern simulation. Television is our strategic site, a gigantic simulator which creates war's virtual reality.

Postmodernism means different things to different people. Through 1980s and 1990s more and more people have become familiar with some form of postmodernism — by taking the high road or the low road. Currently, postmodern thought is entering into a new growth phase linked to the explosion of information and communication technologies, the global mass-media economy of images, the ever increasing determination of many men and women to reconstruct traditional ideas about sex and gender. Though it touches different people in different ways, it is happening to us all. We are all emerging from out of security of our tribes, traditions, religious and world views into a global civilisation.

Postmodernism is obviously connected to the phenomenon of globalisation. Globalisation operates on two fronts—the economic front and the cultural front. The economic front is characterised by multinational capitalism. The cultural front is marked by Western hegemony over the rest of the world's behaviour patterns. It is meaningful to recognise that 'local' and "global' constitute a crude binarism. Roland Robertson uses the term 'globalisation' and defines it as "the creation and incorporation of locality, processes which themselves largely shape, in term, the compression of the world as a whole."[8] Globalisation involves a process of localisation in the interests of the globalising apparatus. It is in the interest of global capitalism to stimulate local market diversity. Both Coca-cola and Sony use the terms. 'Global localisation' to describe the process whereby their products are first embedded and then promoted within the local culture.[9] The global order needs more and more focus on the local at the cost of intermediate strong units like the state. Zygmunt Bauman suggests that "far from acting at cross-purposes and being at war with each other, political fragmentation and economic globalisation are close allies and fellow conspirators."[10] Economic globalisation and political localisation, as Bauman explains, are part of the same process. Multinational capitalism needs a fragmented political order so as to reach every corner of the world. Bauman states:

> For their liberty of movement and for their unconstrained freedom to pursue their ends, global finance, trade and the information industry depend on the political fragmentation —the morcellement—of the world scene.[11]

David Harvey also explains this 'global' phenomenon and shows how to serve the interests of globalisation and multinationalisation, the world can paradoxically become homogenous and fragmented at the same time. He says:

> The shrinkage of space that brings diverse communities across the globe into competition with each other implies localized competitive strategies and a heightened sense of awareness of what makes a place special and gives it competitive advantage. This kind of reaction looks much more strongly to the identification of place, the building and signaling of its unique qualities in an increasingly homogeneous but fragmented world.[12]

Thus, the marginal getting a voice within the dominant discourse, and the local becoming the focus in an increasingly globalised world just to suit the interests of the dominant group. Because of the disjunctive and unstable interplay of commerce, media, national policies and consumer fantasies, ethnicity has now become a global force, forever slipping in and through the cracks between states and borders. Ethnicity is a challenge to the unipolar and hegemonic globalisation. It also leads to fundamentalism and obscurantism. The impulses to globalise and localise are in constant contest. Political fragmentation and economic globalisation are antithetical. They are also complementary to each other. Mike Featherstone argues that globalisation actually produces postmodernism. He says:

> ...the result of growing intensity of contact and communication between nation states and other agencies is to produce a clashing of cultures, which can lead to heightened attempts to draw the boundaries between the self and others. From this perspective the changes which

> are taking place as a result of the current phase of intensified globalization can be understood as provoking reactions that seek to rediscover particularity, localism and difference which generate a sense of the limits of the culturally unifying, ordering and integrating projects associated with western modernity. So, in one sense it can be argued that globalization produces postmodernism.[13]

The postmodern individual is a member of many communities and networks. He is a participant in many discourses and an audience to messages from everybody and everywhere. The messages present conflicting ideals and norms and images of the world-multifrenia. If one turns on a television set and flips randomly from channel to channel, one enters the subculture of another ethnic group, another profession or interest or life style—premodern, modern and postmodern. The postmodern world has four main dimensions—(i) our identity is not formed or fixed by social role or tradition, it is constructed out of many cultural sources, (ii) our morality is not found from a particular cultural or religious heritage. It is forged out of dialogue and choice. Our judgement rests on ever shifting ground of our own socially constructed cultural worldviews. (iii) Our art and culture are eclectic. No style is dominant. People combine traditions, borrow rituals and myths, (iv) Our civilisation is global. It is 'marked by rapid information, exchange and unprecedented mobility. People hold on to their tribal ways and also grab a few of some other tribe's ways. Vaclav Havel states the postmodern phenomenon by means of a symbol:

> For me, a symbol of that state is a Bedouin mounted on a camel and clad in traditional robes under which he is wearing jeans, with a transistor radio in his hands and an ad for coca-cola on the camel's back. No ridicule or shedding tears over the commercial expansion of the west that destroys alien cultures. It is a typical expression of this multi-cultural era, a signal that an amalgamation of cultures is taking place.[14]

Postmodernism views society dividing it into two classes—one produces culture and the other consumes it. The poet or the artist is a powerful producer of culture. Postmodernism is an effort to divest the artist of power by raising the position of the reader or the critic. Hence the importance of the theoretical or critical writing has increased in Europe as well as in the countries of the Third World. Advocating a change in the position of the writer and the critic Derrida observes that the death of the writer implies the participation of the many and democratic manner of deciding cultural values. The writer will cease to impose meaning and write untrue narratives. The developed and developing countries produce culture and sell it to the Third World. Postmodernism is an expression of the decline of bourgeoise culture and the disillusionment of the leftist intellectuals arising from their defeat in 1968.

Postmodernism shares concern with those who because of class, race, gender or sexual preference are others and have been marginalized by the dominant tradition. It offers succour to all those who were oppressed in the past such as women, blacks, the third world and the homosexuals. Postmodernist culture emerges as the culture of egalitarianism which does justice to all. Postmodernism is an effort to protect the interests of all classes and hence it opposes all kinds of domination. Freudianism and Marxism have also been rejected because they are the means of suppression and they oppose multiculturalism. It is necessary for postmodernist multiculturalism that all classes of society may use their own language for self-expression which may be accepted as realistic and true. Some people oppose it on the ground that it will lead to a disintegration of a nation.

Postmodernism is critical of all rigid systems. All systems talk of justice and claim to be fair but oppress an individual. All state powers are alike in their oppressiveness and anti-human approach. Hence postmodernism does not support any power. It says that society is wrong, logic is wrong, organisation is wrong. It is desirable to protect the holy, the mysterious, the dignified inner spirit of man. Foucault is the most precise and powerful critic. From his studies, Foucault comes to the conclusion: a close study of minute politics of power-relations in different places and situations will lead to the conclusion that there is a close relationship between different discourses. Discourses determine the ways and means for social control in places like prison, mental asylum, university, school, college and the psycho-analytic clinic where class interest and class conflict are strengthened layer after layer without any systematic planning. The main complaint of the critics is that post modernists have nothing to do with humanity, human values and the people striving for existence. Their aim is to ruin existing social set up and create a platform for themselves and introduce their philosophy for political gain so that no one may be held responsible for anti-human activities. The relationship between Nietzsche and Hitler, the Nazi relations of Paul de Man known after his death confirm this point. Deconstructive thinkers, like Derrida, Foucault and Paul de Man present a philosophy of indeterminacy or express their helplessness before organisation of power, their humanistic programme carries them towards a new and meaningless anti-human stand. Habermas worries about the angry young man who has anger against establishment and who is eager to destroy everything and the sympathy of the revolutionary thinkers for him cannot be ignored. Twentieth century German History explains Habermas fear about the dangerous postmodern ideology. German Academy was full of anti-modernist views two decades before Nazis came to power.

Anti-postmodernist voices were deepened with the knowledge of Paul de Man's relations with Nazis. Paul de Man was a citizen of Belgium which was then under the rule of Germany. Paul de Man migrated to Germany after the World War II. A research scholar came across a few letters in a library written by de Man in 1940 in support of Nazism. The letters also supported the leftist ideas regarding racial supremacy and the supremacy of the nation over the individual; and the role of Germany in civilising Europe, the acceptance of new world organisation. The anti-Jews views of de Man are extremely dangerous. De Man argued that the contributions of Jews to European literature are insignificant and hence their demand for a separate colony will have no effect on Western literary world. If Jews are sent to Medagaskar or to a separate place in Europe, European culture will lose only a few minor writers and will continue to progress as usual. Today, de Man gives publicity to his anti-humanist theory like deconstruction. A question naturally arises in the minds of the thinkers regarding the rise of Hitler and Mussoliny. The rise of their autocratic rules and their torture of a particular race is obviously the outcome of such ideas. The massacre of Jews is certainly a text to be interpreted indefinitely on deconstructed as appropriate. The history cannot be treated as fiction. It is wrong to see current anti-humanist stand as different from Nazism. Though postmodernist thinkers claim to be staunch critic of contemporary evils like capitalism, totalitarianism, imperialism, colonialism, atrocities on the downtrodden, their theories are akin to the philosophy of Heideggar, a supporter of Hitler and Nazism. Heideggar never denounced the massacre of the Jews nor did he repent his support of Nazism. On account of the gap between their precept and practice, all the declarations of the postmodernists are hollow and are unlikely to bring about any social change. Postmodernism has its influence on Indians also particularly those who are westernised. Postmodernism, like the other ideas of the West, is relevant only for the West. In spite of the talk of equality, the voice of the Third World is nowhere heard. Even today, we are inferior and mean in the eyes of the West. We cannot forget how European thinkers ignore us. Foucault himself expressed his ignorance about the Third World. Postmodernist ideas of social equality, glorification of the region over the universal, the praise of the outlook of the minority community and not the majority community are Euro-centric and feudalistic and inaccessible to the common man. The intellectual has also been commercialised.

Postmodern world is a world of globalised capitalism which depends on the culture of publicity. Media conditions our life in such a manner that TV shows appear to be more real than our actual experience. Political issues are decided by capital. The main problems of the postmodern world are the marginalisation of the others on the basis of class, race gender or sexual preference and the fragmentation of human personality.

Postmodernism glorification of the marginal and the breakdown of the grand narratives make it difficult to develop a consciousness necessary for uniform collective action which may be the basis of common identity, experience and interest. Postmodernism claims to be a radical social principle for our world but its basic features and principles are destructive. Its thinking that there is neither any system nor any history which can be analysed spoils the chance of going into the roots of the forces of exploitation. It also spoils the chance of any serious organised opposition for the sake of human liberation.

Postmodernism rejects the grand narratives of human emancipation and acknowledges that small parts or fragments are desirable for the politics of liberation. It also talks about certain contemporary problems like democracy decentralisation of power, social and economic justice, ecology, women liberation, free sex, human rights, rights of the minorities. But it does not suggest any effective solution. For solution, it is necessary that we should understand material circumstances which stand in the way. It will lead us to capitalism. Here postmodernism is of no help. It is rather a burden. It weakens us to stand in opposition to capitalism.

Jurgen Habermas thinks that if modernity has failed, it is in allowing the totality of life, to be splintered into independent specialties which are left to the narrow competence of experts, while the concrete individual experiences "desublimated meaning' and destructured form' not as a liberation but in the mode of that immense ennui which Baudlaire described over a 'century ago. For Habermas it is not only desirable but also possible to establish a consensus among the participants, in the event of communication. It is logically possible to organise a social formation on more relational terms through a discursively agreed consensus. Habermas pleads for "inter subjective consensus built upon communicative reason."[15] Marxist exponents of humanistic principles, such as Noam Chomsky, Frederick Jameson, Habermas, have argued that humanism holds out the possibility of a rational and universal consensus between responsible individuals with regard to the conceptualisation of a humane, progressive and just social order. In contrast, postmodernist anti-humanists maintain that any universal and normative postulation of rational unanimity is totalitarian and hostile to the challenges of otherness and difference. Lyotard pointed out that the process of reaching consensus is vitiated by a conversational imperialism—the participants in an ethico-political dialogue are rarely equal, and almost never equally represented in the final consensus. The dialogue, is already projected towards some predetermined end such as justice or rationality. The debate between the postmodernist insistence on the impossibility of a universal human nature and the opposing Marxist verdict on the impossibility of a politics which lacks the principle of solidarity remains unresolved.

REFERENCES

I. Linda Hutcheon. *The Poetics of Postmodernism, History. Theory, Fiction* (New York & London: Routledge (1988). p. 10.
2. J. F. Eyotard. The *Postmodern Condition: A Report on Knowledge* (Minneapolis: University of Minnesota Press, 1984). XXIV.
3. Craig Owens. "The Discourse of others: Feminists and Postmodernism" in Hal Poster (ed), *Postmodern Culture* (London and Sydney: Pluto Press), pp. 57-82.
4. Stanley Aronowitz.. "Postmodernism and Politics" in *The Politics of Postmodernism* (ed) Andrew Ross (Minneapolis. 1988). p. 50.
5. Neil Larsen. "Postmodernism and Imperialism: Theory and Politics in Latin America'. *Journal of Literary Criticism* Vol. VI, No. 1 (June. 1993). p. 19.
6. David Harvey. *The Condition of Postmodernity: An Enquiry in the Origin of Cultural Change* (Cambridge: Basil Blackwell. 1989). p. 27.
7. Monroe K. Spears. *Dionysus and the City* (Oxford. 1971). p. 71.
8. Roland Robertson. "Globalization: Time-Space and Homogeneity-Heterogeneity" in Mike Feathcrstone and others (eds) *Global Modernities* (London Sage 1995) p, 40.
9. John Baynon and David Dunkerley (eds) *Globalization: The Reader* (London: The Athlone Press, 2000). p. 20.
10. Zygmunt Bauman. "After the Nation State–What?" in *Globalization: The Human Consequence*: (Cambridge: Polity Press, 1998). 257.
11. *Ibid.*, p. 256.

12. David Harvey. *The Condition of Postmodernity: An Enquiry into Origins of Cultural Change* (Oxford and Cambridge: CA: Sage. 1989), p. 140.

13. Mike Featherstone. "Undoing Culture:" *Globalization: Postmodernism and Identily,* Thousand Oaks. (CA: Sage. 1995). pp. 121-122.

14. Vaclav Havel. "The Search for Meaning in a Global Civilization" in *The Fontana Postmodernism Reader ed.* Walter Trauett (Anderson Fontana Press, 1996). pp. 108-109.

15. Jurgen Habermas. *Irony, Contingency, Solidarity* (Cambridge, 1989), p. 19.

Deconstruction, Marxism and Edward Said

18

Prabin Sinha and R.P. Pradhan

Marxists have criticised deconstruction for ignoring the social and historical dimension of texts or in Saidean terms the worldliness of texts while pursuing a neo-New Critical formalism that antonomises texts and defies rhetoric. Deconstructionists like Christopher Norris in *Deconstruction: Theory and Practice*, who consider Marxism as antithetical to deconstruction accuse Marxists of being 'dogmatic totalizers or naive referentialists who regulate the liberal freedom of reference by pinning it down to one meaning or one referent in the extra-textual world'[1]. For the Marxists, deconstructionists are guilty of an irrationalist mystification that demolishes that rational basis necessary for a criticism of capitalism and for the construction of a rational society.

I

Deconstruction has been variously interpreted as (a) the attempt of an ineffectual bourgeois intelligentia to reduce the worlds' action to its own inaction; (b) the attempt of a critical power group to take over the realm of cultural discourse from the artists traditionally honoured in it; (c) the attempts of this ineffectual bourgeois intelligentia to fend off a real Marxism by rendering all discourse ineffectual, and thereby perpetuate the present in which it weaves its fantasies before a credulous audience; or (d) simple sabotage—the genuine efforts of a Marxist intelligentia to undermine Western discourse as a whole and discredit the monuments of Western culture.

Deconstruction emerged from the writings of Jacques Derrida which are detailed and difficult interpretations of the writings of major philosophers—Plato, Kant, Rousseau, Hegel, Husserl, Heidegger—and are close readings of these philosophers' writings. From the close readings of these philosophers, Derrida tries to show how a philosophical position is subverted or undone by its own blind-spots or "aporias". Western thinking is based on what Derrida calls "logocentrism", the assumption that there is an order of meaning, truth, logic, logos, which serve as a foundation. This assumption emerges in hierarchical distinctions such as meaning/form, literal/figurative, transcendental/empirical, positive/negative, where the first is seen as prior or fundamental, and the second seen as a derivation or manifestation of the first. When thinking about language we take the serious, literal statements as the norm and consider figurative or metaphorical assertions and non-serious utterances as deviations from the standard cases. This logocentrism is so ingrained in our system of thought that all metaphysicians have proceeded from it, from Plato to Rousseau, Kant to Hegel, Descartes to Husserl: good before evil, the positive before the negative, the pure before the impure and so on. These hierarchical distinctions structure our most elementary thinking. Therefore, it is not possible to bring an end to metaphysics but we cannot also continue to rely on those hierarchical oppositions of metaphysics with the same confidence. Deconstruction does not negate metaphysics nor seek the end of metaphysics but attempts to produce dislocations of these hierarchical structures by exploring how they are subverted by the very texts and arguments that rely on them.

In "White Mythology", for example, Derrida approaches the hierarchical relationship between the literal and the figurative or metaphorical and shows that the treatment of the literal as basic and the figurative as derivative is an unwarranted imposition. Derrida shows that the literal can be taken as the special case of the metaphorical rather than vice-versa; metaphoricity or seeing things in terms of another, is the very basis of conceptualisation. As Neitzsche says, 'Every idea originates through equating the unequal'[2] and again, 'A nerve-stimulus, first transcribed (ubertragen) into an image (Bild)! First metaphor ! The image again copied into a sound ! Second metaphor ! And each time he (the creator of language) leaps completely out of one sphere right into the midst of an entirely different one.'[3]

Similarly, we can demonstrate the imposition of various hierarchies in our thought process which metaphysics has systematically and gradually achieved. This undoing of philosophical oppositions seems to have little direct bearing on literary criticism but there are serious implications of using deconstructive tools in criticism. By disrupting the hierarchical relationships in which oppositions like philosophy and literature, literal and figurative, intrinsic and extrinsic, form and meaning, representation and the represented, signifier and signified, have functioned, deconstruction makes reading and interpretation the process of questioning, investigating and not taking for granted. So much for deconstruction in literary criticism. We can now look into the role of deconstruction in socio-political and ethical matters.

As mentioned earlier, Derrida's deconstruction has been variously interpreted and its role in society and politics ascribed various names. Derrida himself has been taken as the philosopher of the bourgeois and later also as one who has concurred with Marxists in his criticism, however oblique, of the 'New World Order' premised on the values of unbridled corporate capitalism and "liberal democracy, U.S. style"[4]. Derrida's *Specters of Marx* shows Derrida's denunciations of the massive injustice and violence which characterise the present global (U.S. dominated) distribution of resources and human rights. Derrida's detractors club him with capitalist ideologues like Francis Fukuyama as they think that his ideas of *difference* and *supplementarity* exert a dislocating pressure on the logocentric craving for actuality, presence, and transparent proximity to self in the speaking voice.

Habermas takes Derrida to have simply sabotaged the entire enlightenment project through his critique of Western metaphysical philosophical tradition with its roots in phono-logocentrism. Unlike post-structuralists and post-modernists who dismiss such ideas (Enlightenment idea) *tout court* as just a surreptitious pretext for carrying on in the same old way, Derrida's deconstructive reading of texts keeps faith in the vigil of enlightenment critique despite pressing hard on its internal pressures and moments of self-induced aporia. Derrida's deconstructive reading is a patient and meticulous thinking through—an 'immanent' critique of metaphysics which cannot be carried on except by means of those various metaphysical concepts and categories which belong to that same history of thought which deconstruction both inhabits and sets out to challenge at those points where its presuppositions come most visibly under strain.

Derrida's disciples are responsible for attaching a sense to the term metaphysical that can be said to be pejorative. In his essay, "The Marxism Deconstruction Debate in literary Criticism", Michael Ryan points out that the formalism prevalent in literary criticism asserting the indecidability of meaning and rhetoricity of texts is the result of primarily two operations of the Yale school critics—'their focusing and limiting of his (Derrida's) critical philosophy to the professional and institutional requisites of literary criticism and their ignoring of his political leftism in favour of the pluralism that is one dominant ideology of the American academy'[5]. Michael Ryan says that the Yale school can be held responsible for shunting aside the social and political possibilities of Derrida's texts. Not surprisingly, those texts in French where Derrida does deal with institutional questions remain for the most part untranslated.

However, deconstruction has something to offer to Marxist political criticism, that is, a criticism that directly relates critical reading to social problems. 'Political criticism is a necessary consequence of the interaction of deconstructive philosophy and Marxist literary theory, for what that interaction shows is that discursive operations in texts cannot be declared another to a real presence or substance in society; social life is itself constituted as a network...of representations, relations and discursive practices. Social meaning, like literary textual meaning, is constructed by representations and discourses; it is not of the nature of a pre-discursive "truth" that appears in an unmediated luminousness to the mind'[6].

Marxist literary critics are right in saying that textual aporias are to be referred to social contradictions but it is equally true that *social ideology has a rhetorical dimension* the revelation of which can be directly useful to the Marxists. It is in the domain of cultural criticism that deconstruction seems most relevant to the critique of ideology. It is ideology that produces class, race and sex domination and which induces a false sense of reality on the part of the dominated people. In an inegalitarian society where disparities should engender conflict and trigger revolutions, ideology works to make inequality seem natural and eternal and thus makes legitimate the use of force against those who tend to violate the 'natural' and 'eternal' inequality. Thus, with the help of police power, ideology prevents material tensions and institutional exploitation from erupting into revolutions. The argument here is that ideology makes the social world seem natural and endowed with a self-evident truth value.

Our delusion with ideology (with its self-evident truth value) is similar to the entire Western metaphysical delusion with speech with its own self-evident truth value which arises from 'hearing ourselves speak'. This phonologocentrism posits a 'presence' which is not present, similar to the 'presence' of a 'natural' social world which too is not present. Derrida shows that phonocentrism is deluded in its belief that speech if more originary than writing and similarly ideology deludes us into believing that social reality is more originary than its representation in ideology.

> 'Cultural representations in the media or in clothing symbolism for example, are supposedly secondary appendages to or expressions of this pre-existent reality, women are women, for example, prior to the clothing they wear; they have a natural self identical being, characterized by passivity among other things, that exists prior to its expression or representation through clothing. Similarly, when the news media describes the United States as "free", it is supposedly representing in language a pre-existing reality, whose truth is in no way dependent on such secondary representation as words'[7].

What deconstruction suggests to us is that the 'self-evident truth' of ideology may be the result of strategies of representation. What supposedly comes second in our (mis)apprehension of reality may in fact determine what is supposedly primary.

Perhaps women may not be what they supposedly already are—passive social beings—if they were not represented in a certain way in our culture and if they did not adopt or wear certain symbolic representations that actively constitute them as passive, weak, vulnerable. The free-market ideology that dominates global economy which in turn is dominated by the United States constantly represents the world guided by market forces as 'free'. Perhaps, it needs to constantly reiterate its 'freedom' to continue the oppressive economic structure it promotes. When the President of the United States says that the 'free World' is threatened by Iranian adventure in nuclear technology, he is stating the ideology that finds it just to delimit nuclear technology to a few states which are 'sane' and 'safe' to the world. The so called 'rogue' states may just be states which are seeking their own development quite similar to the states of the so called 'free World'. What is implied here is that representations play the vital role in constructing social reality and the role of ideology is to occlude the role of representation so that the socially manufactured social reality seems natural.

What deconstructive criticism does is point out the way representations and discourses actively construct the social world rather than merely represent it. The major assumption here is that cultural representations are not simply accessories to economic, political and social power but in today's electronic media dominated representations, cultural representations are much more potent. One only has to remind himself of the fact that one strand in the progress of civilisation has consisted of replacing the bayonet with the school system and the media.

Deconstructive criticism has questioned the unity of texts, the veracity of truth and posited the free play of signifiers or in Barbara Johnson's words 'the warring forces of signification in a text'. This has had a salutary impact on social cultural criticism. History now is not a unity—various strands start out competing against each other in a nation's history. In the realm of cultural studies, it has opened a veritable Pandora's box and gone are the days of universality and cross cultural consensus. In India, where there are various divisions and strata in society according to class, caste, religion, language, ethnicity, sex and so on, the question of an official history is problematic with each group asserting its voice and a confluence of these various histories is difficult to come by. Writing history is now a more democratic process with the assimilation of varied voices.

II

Edward Said's criticism unites many strands—Marxist concern with the downtrodden, deconstruction's notion of the 'other', Foucault's theory of discourse and power as also the question of representation which is the central concern of any critical theory. Said's *Orientalism* is regarded as the catalyst which brought the world (circumstantial reality) with a bang in literary criticism and in the words of Homi Bhabha, 'dramatically shifts the locus of contemporary theory from the Left Bank to the West Bank and beyond...'[8].

Said is vehement against the Enlightenment conception of man with its prescriptivist notion of adult rationality which has a history of exclusion and subsequent oppression. The Kantian conception of Enlightenment as taking man from a condition of immaturity to adulthood, rationality has a history of exclusion and subsequent oppression. The Kantian conception of Enlightenment as taking man from a condition of immaturity to adulthood, rationality and maturity, restricts the reflection of heterogeneous human existence to the normative condition of adult rationality, which Said argues, is itself a value arising from the specific historicity of European societies. Proceeding from the Kantian conception of the Enlightenment and its product 'man', the possibility of taking cognizance of other ways of being human is precluded. As a corollary, it follows that those who are not rational, mature, adult, are not human. The imperialist and ethnocentric hierarchy between European rationality, adulthood and colonial irrationality, immaturity, childishness, stems from the Kantian conception of Enlightenment which gives a prescription of man, deviation from which leads to being denied the status of man. For this position, it is not difficult to see the colonial 'civilising mission' or '*mission civilisatrice*'.

Edward Said looks into the ways that imperialists used to express the relation between Europe and its 'other'—the Oriental is 'irrational', depraved (fallen), childlike, "different", thus the European is rational, mature, "normal"[9]. Post colonial theory (Edward Said) recognises that "colonial discourse typically rationalises itself through rigid oppositions such as maturity/ immaturity, civilisation/barbarism, developed/ developing, progressive/primitive"[10]. Like Derrida's deconstruction, Said's post-colonialism dismantles this hierarchy and reveals that Orientalist discourse or the ideology of imperialism is the result of the convergence of anthropocentrism and Europocentrism. This dismantling of hierarchies, imposed on our thought process through ideology, subverts the claims of absoluteness of cultural norms. The dominant culture becomes one more sub-culture, one that has the power to impose itself generally. The deconstruction of the network of representations and discursive practices creates an opening in the apparent closure of self-sufficient meaning or truth, be it philosophical or cultural.

Said's dismantling of the hierarchies of Orientalist discourse creates possibilities for a plural culture—one that is not bound by normative and prescriptive notion of Enlightenment adult human rationality. European culture becomes one more subculture which with the aid of power (economic, military and discursive) had imposed itself as the normative culture.

Said uses the tools of deconstruction in dismantling the myth of the eternal, timeless and changeless Orient and he uses Marxist notions of economic power which gives the West its power to represent. Said is not averse to using Marxist notions of economic and political power but he certainly has reservations regarding the privilege given to economy over culture and its representations. As we have argued, cultural representations are not merely secondary accessories to economic and political power; they have the power to support and sustain and in some cases even originate the exercise of illegitimate power. In today's world of electronic media dominated representations, world powers use the news media to churn out representations which create world opinion and help sustain the dominance of the leading economic and political powers on the world map.

We can say of Said that he uses both Marxist and deconstructive tools for critiquing Western imperialism. Though Said criticises Marx for his ethnocentric view and theory in his book *Orientalism*, he cannot deny that Marxism delivers theoretically, a set of categories that we can work with, through which we might understand ourselves and our implications in the history of European/capitalist imperialism differently. Moreover, as Gayatri Chakraborty Spivak repeatedly argues, it is profoundly enabling to rethink the present relationship between the 'first' and the 'third' world through Marxist accounts of the globalisation of capital and the international division of labour. Said uses both Marxist and deconstructive tools in his critique of the ideology of European/capitalist imperialism. He conflates deconstructive anti-humanism and Marxist humanism in his critique of Orientalism. Though, he gets himself in a difficult theoretical position by trying to unite the tenets of two seemingly incompatible theories (as his critics like Robert Young point out), we can appreciate his contribution to cultural criticism by placing him in a position where deconstruction intersects with Marxism.

References:

1. Ryan, Michael. (1984) "The Marxism Deconstruction Debate in Literary Theory", in *Journal of Literary Criticism*, Vol. 1, no. 2, ed. Rajnath, New Delhi, p. 53.
2. Spivak, Gayatri Chakraborty 1994. (1976) Translator's Preface to *Of Grammatology*, Motilal Banarsidas, Delhi, p. (xxii).
3. *Ibid*, p. (xxii).
4. Norris, Christopher 1991. (1982) *Deconstruction: Theory and Practice*, Routledge, London, p. 5.
5. Ryan, Michael. (1984) "The Marxism Deconstruction Debate in Literary Theory", in *Journal of Literary Criticism*, Vol. 1, no. 2, ed. Rajnath, New Delhi, p. 58
6. *Ibid*, 59
7. *Ibid*, 60
8. Gandhi, Leela. (1998) *Post-Colonial Theory*, Oxford University Press, Delhi, p. 73.
9. Said, Edward, W. (1979) *Orientalism*, Vintage, New York, p. 40.
10. Gandhi, Leela. (1998) *Post-Colonial Theory*, Oxford University Press, Delhi, p. 32.

Homi Bhabha As a Postcolonial Critic

19

Deepak Kumar Singh

Indians have contributed to postcolonial discourse in a substantial way. Apart from Edward Said, Gayatri Chakravorty Spivak and Homi Bhabha are the other forces that have shaped this discourse. Postcolonial criticism has not simply enlarged the traditional field of English studies, or refocused attention on neglected aspects or areas; it has also significantly altered the modes of analysis which were dominant within the discipline during the period 1945 to 1980. Most notably, perhaps, it has helped to undermine the traditional conception of disciplinary boundaries. Postcolonial critics have characteristically worked to break down formerly fixed boundaries between text and context in order to show the continuities between patterns of representation of subject, people and material practices of (neo-) colonial power. Postcolonialism is not merely a chronological label referring to the period after the demise of empires. It is ideologically an emancipatory concept[1], particularly for the students of literature outside Western world, because it makes us interrogate many aspects of the study of literature that we were made to take for granted, enabling us not only to read our own texts in our own terms, but also to re-interpret some of the old canonical texts from Europe from the perspective of our specific historical and geographical location. It also brings severely into question the old idea of the autotelic nature[2] of literary text and "the sealed antiseptic" notion of "artistic" value uncontaminated by the political circumstances of its production and reception—forcing everyone involved in the discipline to rethink the limitations of the Eurocentric/ Universalistic aesthetic norms.

In fact, the most significant effect of postcolonial criticism is to further undermine the universalistic claims once made on behalf of literature by liberal humanist critics. If we claim that great literature has a timeless and universal significance we thereby demote or disregard cultural, social, regional, and national differences in experience and outlook, preferring instead to judge all literature by a single, supposedly 'universal', standard. For centuries, the European colonising powers have devalued the nations past, seeing its pre-colonial era as a pre-civilised limbo, or even as a historical void. Children, both black and white, have been taught to see history, culture and progress as beginning with the arrival of the Europeans. If the first step towards a postcolonial perspective is to reclaim one's past, then the second is to begin to erode the colonialist ideology by which that past has been devalued. Theories of colonial discourses have been hugely influential in the development of postcolonialism. They explore the ways that 'representations' and 'modes of perception' are used as fundamental weapons to keep colonised people subservient to colonial rule. Many writers have striven to demonstrate how colonialism suggests certain ways of seeing, specific modes of understanding the world and one's place in it, that assist in justifying the subservience of colonised people to the "superior", civilised order of the Western colonizers. These ways of seeing are at the root of the study of colonial discourses. Colonialism is perpetuated in part by justifying to those in the colonising nation the idea that it is right and proper to rule over other people, and by getting colonised people to accept their lower ranking in the colonial order of things—a process we can call "colonising the mind."

Colonialism has taken many different forms and has engendered diverse effects around the world. Denis Judd[3] argues that none can doubt that the desire for profitable trade, plunder and enrichment was the primary force that led to the establishment of the imperial structure. Hence, Colonialism and Capitalism share a mutually supportive relationship with each other. "Colonialism" is sometimes used interchangeably with "Imperialism", but in truth the terms mean different things. As

Peter Childs and Patrick Williams argue[4], Imperialism is an ideological concept which upholds the legitimacy of the economic and military control of one nation by another. Colonialism, however, is only one form of practice which results from the ideology of imperialism and specifically concerns the settlement of one group in a new location. Imperialism is not strictly concerned with the issue of settlement; it does not demand the settlement of different places in order to work. They define 'Imperialism' as the extension and expansion of trade and commerce under the protection of political, legal, and military controls. Benita Parry considers colonialism as "a specific, mutable states, one which preceded the rule of international finance capitalism and whose formal ending Imperialism has survived."[5]

One important antecedent for postcolonialism was the growth of the study of commonwealth literature. "Commonwealth literature" was a term literary critics began to use to describe literatures in English emerging from a selection of countries with a history of colonialism. It incorporated the study of writers from the predominantly European settler communities, as well as writers belonging to those countries which were in process of gaining independence from British rule, such as those from the African, Caribbean and South-Asian nations. The shift from "Colonial" to "Commonwealth" perhaps suggests a particular version of history in which the status of colonised countries happily changes from subservience to equality. Commonwealth literature may well have been created in an attempt to bring together writings from around the world on an equal footing, yet the assumption remained that these texts were addressed primarily to a Western English-speaking readership. The "Commonwealth" in "Commonwealth literature" was never fully free from the older, more imperious connotations of the term.

Theories of colonial discourses have been hugely influential in the development of postcolonialism. They explore the ways that representations and modes of perception are used as fundamental weapons of colonial power to keep colonised people subservient to colonial rule. Colonialism operates by persuading people to internalise its logic and speak its language; to perpetuate the values and assumptions of the colonisers as regards the way they perceive and represent the world. Theories of colonial discourses call attention to the role language plays in getting people succumb to a particular way that results in the kind of situation. Colonial discourses form the intersections where language and power meet. Language is more than simply a means of communications; it constitutes our world-view by cutting up and ordering reality into meaningful units.

Homi Bhabha has examined questions of identity, social agency and national affiliations and in doing this he has provided a theory of cultural hybridity and the "translation" of social difference which goes beyond the polarities of Self and Other, East and West. In a dazzling series of essays, he explains why the culture of Western modernity must be relocated from the postcolonial perspective. The republication of Bhabha's essays in *The Location of Culture*[6] has greatly facilitated reconsideration of his contribution to contemporary analysis of the cultural and political issues raised by (neo-) colonialism, race, ethnicity and migration. When we consider these series of essays as a developing body of work, rather than a series of discreet articles published in different journals which are widely dispersed in different disciplinary and geographical locations, it becomes much easier to appreciate the degree to which Bhabha challenges the vision of his predecessors in the postcolonial field and those of Frantz Fanon and Edward Said in particular. Whereas Said's *Orientalism*[7] focuses on the Middle-East, Bhabha's particular interest is in the cultural exchanges involved in the history of British rule in India. Bhabha's discussion of postcoloniality assumes a relationship of continuity rather than rupture between the era of colonialism and the contemporary period, which he refers to as "the on-going colonial present."[8]

The lack of conviction within colonial discourses is also the concern of Homi Bhabha. The purpose of looking at Bhabha's work is to construct a working knowledge of his concepts of "ambivalence" and "mimicry" in the operations of colonial discourses. Let's take "ambivalence" first. Like Edward Said, Bhabha argues that colonialism is informed by a series of assumptions which aim to legitimate its view of other lands and people. "The objective of colonial discourses", writes Bhabha "is to construe the colonised as a population of degenerate types on the basis of racial origin, in order to justify conquests and to establish systems of administration and instruction." However, in an inspired departure from Said's concept of Orientalism, Bhabha argues that this important aim is never fully met. This is because the "discourse of colonialism" does not function according to plan because it is always pulling in two contrary directions at once.

On the one hand, the discourse of colonialism would have it that the "orient" is a radically strange creature whose bizarre and eccentric nature is the cause for both curiosity and concern. The colonised are considered the "other" of the Westerner (or the colonising subject), as they are essentially outside Western culture and civilisation. Yet, on the other hand, the discourse of colonialism attempts to domesticate colonised subjects and abolish their radical "otherness", by bringing them inside Western understanding through the orientalist project of constructing knowledge about them. Hence, in Bhabha's term, "colonial discourse produces the colonised as a social reality which is at once an "other" and yet entirely knowable and visible."[10] The colonisers never admit that other peoples are not really very different from themselves, as this would undercut the legitimacy of colonialism.

Probing Said's argument that Western representations of the East are based primarily on fantasies, desires and imaginings, Bhabha points out that the fantasies of the colonial stereotype often appear as horrors. The discourse of colonialism is frequently populated with "terrifying stereotypes of savagery, cannibalism, lust and anarchy."[11] Any attempt to subdue, says Bhabha, the radical otherness of the colonized subjects is perpetually offset by the alarming fantasies that are projected into them. This indicates how, in the discourse of colonialism, colonised subjects are split between contrary positions. They are domesticated, harmless, and knowable; but also at the same time wild, harmful, and mysterious. Bhabha argues that, as a consequence, in colonialist representations the colonised subject is always in motion, sliding ambivalently between the polarities of similarity and difference; he or she will not stand still.

Bhabha further suggests that because of this slippery motion, stereotypes are deployed as a means to arrest the ambivalence of the colonised subjects by describing him or her in static terms. But this fixing of colonised subject's position always fails to secure the colonised subject into place. As Bhabha argues, "the same old stories of the Negro's animality, the Coolie's inscrutability or the stupidity of the Irish must be told (compulsively) again and afresh, and are differently gratifying and terrifying each time."[12] The repetition of the colonial stereotype is an attempt to secure the colonised in a fixed position, but also an acknowledgement that this can never be achieved.

In his essay, "Of Mimicry and Man: The Ambivalence of Colonial Discourse," Bhabha builds on these ideas and explores how the ambivalence of the colonised subject becomes a direct threat to the authority of the colonisers through the effects of "mimicry". He describes mimicry as "one of the most elusive and effective strategies of colonial power and knowledge."[13] He focuses on the fact that in colonised nations such as India, the British authorities required the native people to work on their behalf and thus had to teach them the English language. These figures, comparable to Fanon's French-educated colonials depicted in *Black Skin, White Masks*, described as "mimic men" who learn to act English but do not look English nor are accepted as such. As Bhabha puts it, "to be Anglicised is emphatically not to be English."[14]

However, these mimic men are not to be disempowered, slavish individuals required by the British in India. Bhabha argues that they are invested with the power to menace the colonisers because they threaten to disclose the ambivalence of the discourse of colonialism which the use of stereotypes anxiously tries to conceal. Hearing their language returning through the mouths of the colonised, the colonisers are faced with the worrying threat of resemblance between colonisers and colonised. This threatens to collapse the orientalist structure of knowledge, in which such oppositional distinctions are made.

The ambivalent position of the colonized mimic men in relation to the colonisers—"almost the same but not quite"[15]—is, in Bhabha's thinking, a source of anti-colonial resistance in that it presents an unconquerable challenge of the entire structure of the discourse of colonialism. By speaking English (or the coloniser's language), the colonised have not succumbed to the power of the coloniser. Contrary to the belief, they challenge the representations which attempt to fix and define them. In this sense, "mimicry" has become the new slogan of postcolonial literary analysis.

In fact, "Sly Civility" also illustrates some more basic ways in which colonialism fragments the coloniser's identity and authority. The argument is advanced primarily through analysis of the contradictory career of the representative nineteenth-century figure, J.S. Mill. Bhabha points out that one of Mill's most famous essays, "On Liberty", was actually written in response to Macaulay's proposals for the reform of Indian education. Mill attempts to make domestic democracy compatible with overseas despotism, in a unified vision of Britain's identity and mission as a nation. In Bhabha's view, however, this generates only "an agnostic uncertainty" which "puts on trail the very discourse of civility within which representative government claims its liberty and empire its ethics".[16] The radical contradictions in nineteenth-century British discourses of the nation are typified, for Bhabha, in Macaulay's essay on Warren Hastings, which explains the principles of government espoused by the East India Company in the following manner: "Be the father and the oppressor of the people; be just and unjust, moderate and rapacious".[17] In "Sly Civility", subaltern resistance is figured in terms of the native's refusal to satisfy the coloniser's demand for recognition. Faced with this elusive Anglicised colonised subject, who inhabits a multiplicity of subject-positions, "in-between" Englishness and an "original" Indianness, the demand of colonial authority can neither unify its message nor readily place its subjects. In fact, Bhabha's most important contribution has been to stress that colonialism is not a one-way street, that because it involves an interaction between colonisers and colonised, the coloniser is as much affected by its systems as the colonised.

Bhabha's another essay, "DissemiNation: Time, Narrative and Margins of the Modern Nation"[18] reveals nationalistic representations as highly unstable and fragile constructions which cannot even produce the unity they promise. This is because, in Bhabha's argument, they become split by similar kinds of ambivalence to those that threaten the coherence of colonial discourses. In making this argument, the essay might make us think about the worrying similarities between colonial discourses and nationalistic representations.

In fact, the aim of the nationalistic discourses is to create community out of difference, to convert the "many into one". In so doing, Bhabha argues, they engage with two contradictory modes of representation, which he calls the "pedagogic" and the "performative", each possessing its own relationship with time. Nationalistic discourses are split by a disruptive "double narrative movement".[19] On the one hand, nationalism is a "pedagogic" discourse. It claims a fixed origin for the nation and asserts a sense of a continuous history which links the nation's people in the present to previous generations of national subjects. Further, it is "pedagogical" because it warrants the authority, legitimacy and primacy of the nation as the central political and social unit which collects the population into a "people". The people are the object of pedagogical discourse; they are the body which nationalism constructs and upon which it acts. Pedagogical narratives are shaped by a "continuist, accumulative temporality",[20] which gives the impression of the steady, linear movement of time from past to present to future—as in the narrative of the nation's history.

But on the other hand, Bhabha argues that nationalistic discourses are simultaneously "performative". This term refers to the way in which nationalistic icons and popular signs are continually rehearsed by the people in order to keep secure the sense of "deep, horizontal comradeship". A national culture, argues Bhabha, must be endlessly performed; the arbitrary range of symbols which it uses to forge unity require repeated inscription as the stuff of national significance—"the scraps, patches and rags of daily life must be repeatedly turned into the signs of a coherent national culture".[21] Thus, the people are also the subject of nationalist discourses, actively involved in the (re)production of its signs and traditions: they must repeatedly tell their history, perform the nation's rituals, celebrate its great figures and commemorate its anniversaries. Hence, nationalist discourses in their performative aspects function under a different temporality, the "repetitious" and "recursive."[22]

As a consequence of this "double" narrative movement, the nation is split by what Bhabha terms the "conceptual ambivalence"[23] at the heart of its discursive strategies. The nation is always being pulled between two incompatible opposites: the nation as a fixed, originary essence (continuist and pedagogical), and the nation as a socially manufactured and devoid of a fixed origin (repetitive and performative). Between these two positions, out this "disjunctive temporality"[24] a sense of nation's homogeneous "people" begin to fragment. In fact, Bhabha's essay tries to communicate that there can never be any one, coherent, common narrative through which a nation and its people can be adequately captured. The nation remains a site of heterogeneity and difference. Narratives which claim otherwise can do so only through the marginalisation of certain groups, yet even this claim will be undone by the "disjunctive temporalities" which they cannot help but create. In Bhabha's work, nationalist discourses are ultimately illiberal and must always be challenged.

Homi Bhabha, himself a migrant from Bombay to Britain who now lives in America, advocated new and exciting ways of thinking about identity born from "the great history of the languages and landscapes of migration and diasporas."[25] Bhabha describes these experiences as new forms of postcolonial identity, making a slippage between 'migrant' and 'postcolonial' which is not free from problems. Bhabha's essay addresses those who live 'border lives' on the margins of different nations, in-between contrary homelands. Borders are important thresholds, full of contradiction and ambivalence. They both separate and join different places. They are intermediate locations where one contemplates moving beyond a barrier. For Bhabha, the border is the place where conventional patterns of thought are disturbed and can be disturbed by the possibility of crossing. At the border, past and present, inside and outside no longer remain separated as binary opposites but instead commingle and conflict. So, it is argued that imaginative border-crossings are as much a consequence of migration as the physical crossing of borders.

NOTES AND REFERENCES

1. Meenakshi Mukherjee. "Interrogating Post-colonialism", *Interrogating Post-colonialism: Theory, Text and Context* (ed.), Harish Trivedi and Meenakshi Mukherjee (Shimla: I.I.A.S.Rashtrapati Nivas, 2000), p.l.
2. *Ibid.*, p.2.
3. John McLeod. "From Commonwealth to Postcolonial", *Beginning Postcolonialism* (Manchester: Manchester University Press, 2000), p.7.
4. *Ibid.*
5. Benita Parry. "Problems in Current Theories of Colonial Discourse" *Oxford Literary Review* (Vol.9, Nos.l and 2, 1987), p.34.
6. Homi Bhabha. *The Location of Culture* (London: Routledge, 1994).
7. Edward Said. *Orientalism* (London: Routledge, 1978).
8. Homi Bhabha. "Articulating the Archaic: Cultural Difference and Colonial Nonsense", *The Location of Culture*, p. 128.
9. Homi Bhabha. "The Other Question; Stereotype, Discrimination and the Discourse of Colonialism", *The Location of Culture*, p. 70.
10. *Ibid.*, p.70-71.
11. *lbid.*, p.72.
12. *Ibid.*, p.77.
13. Homi Bhabha. "Of Mimicry and Man: The Ambivalence of Colonial Discourse", *The Location of Culture*, p.85.
14. *Ibid.*, p.87.
15. *Ibid.*, p.89.
16. Homi Bhabha. "Sly Civility", *The Location of Culture*, p. 96.
17. Macaulay quoted in Bhabha's, "Sly Civility", *The Location of Culture*, p. 95.
18. Homi Bhabha. "DissemiNation; Time, Narrative and the Margins of the Modern Nation", *The Location of Culture*, pp. 139-170.
19. *Ibid.*, p. 145.
20. *Ibid.*

21. *Ibid.*
22. *Ibid.*
23. *Ibid.*, p. 146.
24. *Ibid.*, p. 148.
25. Homi Bhabha. "How Newness Enters the World: Postmodern Space, Postcolonial Times and the Trails of Cultural Translation", *The Location of Culture*, p. 235.

Contributors

A.N. Dwivedi is a former Professor of English in the University of Allahabad. He is a scholar, poet, critic and a writer of more than three dozen books.

K.M. Pandey Senior Professor of English in B.H.U. has authored several books.

Anju Mishra is a Senior Lecturer in C.M.P. College, Allahabad.

Banibrata Mahanta is an upcoming scholar and critic. Presently he is a senior lecturer in Dept. of English, B.H.U., Varanasi.

O.P. Dwivedi is a guest lecturer in the University of Allahabad.

Negendra Kumar has authored a number of books and is presently Professor in I.I.T., Roorkee.

Sanjay Swarnkar is a senior Reader in C.S.J.M. University, Kanpur.

Neeru Tandon is a Senior Reader in V.S.S.D. College, Kanpur.

Sanjit Mishra is a Senior Lecturer in M.S.J. College, Rajasthan.

Sarvajit Mukherjee is a Senior Reader in Dept. of English in the University of Allahabad.

Susmita Bhattacharya is a Senior Reader in Dept. of English in D.D.U. Gorakhpur University.

Supriya Shukla is H.O.D. of English in V.S.S.D. College, Kanpur.

G. Rai, H.O.D. of English in Gorakhpur University, is scholar and critic. He has written several books on Indian English Literature.

Sunita Rai is a lecturer in Arya Mahila College, Varanasi.

R.N. Rai Senior Professor of English in B.H.U. has authored three books on Indian English Drama.

Prabin Sinha is H.O.D. of English in D.A.V. College, Gorakhpur.

D.K. Singh is a Senior lecturer in Dept. of English, D.A.V. College, Lucknow.

R.P. Pradhan is a senior Assistant Professor in V.S.S.D. College. He has authored two books.

Kavita Shukla is lecturer in PSIT, Kanpur.